Laramie Junior High
1355 N 22nd
Laramie, WY 82070

Western Asia

Library of Congress Number: 88-18337

2 3 4 5 6 7 8 9 0 97 96 95 94 93 92

Library of Congress Cataloging-in-Publication Data

Klandorf, Hillar, 1953-
[Asia occidentale. English]
Western Asia / Hillar Klandorf.

— (World nature encyclopedia)
Translation of: Asia occidentale.
Includes index.
Summary: Describes the plant and animal life of western Asia and its interaction with the environment.
1. Ecology—Middle East—Juvenile literature. 2. Biotic communities—Middle East—Juvenile literature.
[1. Ecology—Middle East. 2. Middle East.]
I. Title. II. Series: Natura nel mondo. English.
QH179.K5313 1988 574.5'264'0956—dc19 88-18383
ISBN 0-8172-3325-3

WORLD NATURE ENCYCLOPEDIA

Western Asia

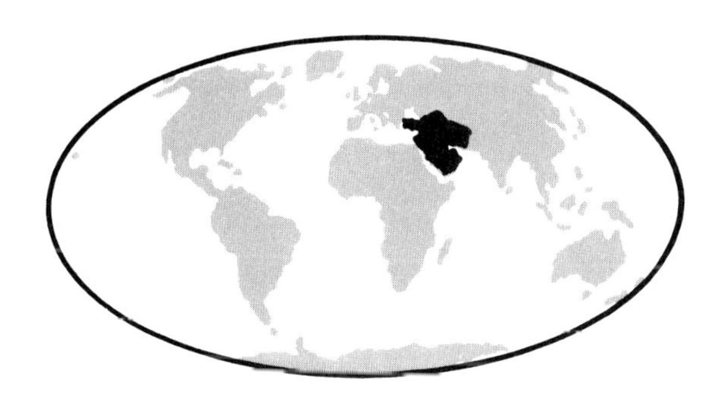

Hillar Klandorf

RAINTREE
STECK-VAUGHN
LIBRARY
Austin, Texas

CONTENTS

INTRODUCTION

From the air, western Asia resembles another planet whose surface is an empty expanse. Here and there, oil drilling rigs come into view, rising like strange, flaming monuments in the void.

Asia, the largest continent in the world, stretches from the Mediterranean Sea on the west to the far eastern lands of India and China. Sand, rocks, and barren mountains with occasional stretches of yellow grass appear almost continuously on its landscape. Throughout the last few thousand years, the desert has continued to expand, leaving its inhabitants in a continual search for new ways to survive.

This was the land of the Assyrians, the Babylonians, the Medians, the Persians, the Jews, the Arabs, the Afghans, and Kazaks. They all occupied this soil for a time, found fertile locations and worked hard to make a living. They knew difficult times as well. They experienced war and exile and each day fought the relentless advance of the desert.

At times it was Asians who invaded Europe. Militades's troops met the Persians in battle on the fields of Marathon, in Greece, in 490 B.C. Charles Martel fought the Arabs at

Poitiers in France, in A.D. 732. When Europeans drove back the Asians in battle, they were not only protecting their life, liberty, and well being from invading troops. They were also fighting large groups of people who were searching for new lands because their own was becoming a desert.

Today modern technology has helped to make those dusty lands livable. Beneath the surface of the desert, great stores of oil have been discovered. Some of the profits from the sale of the oil have been used to remove salt from the sea water, to construct skyscrapers and highways, and to produce fruit and vegetables using new methods of irrigation. However, because the dry area continues to expand and because people continue to hunt and kill the few animals that are adapted to living in this harsh environment, the land is still largely desert.

Western Asia today is a land of contrasts. While it is vast and rich in some resources, such as oil, it is also a wilderness where survival is always a challenge. In spite of its dangers, western Asia is a fascinating land to explore through travel or through the pages of a book.

THE GREAT ASIAN DESERTS

Preceding page: Kuci nomads set up camp near the border of a desert area in western Afghanistan.

Opposite: A desolate stretch of desert is seen in northern Iran at the border of the Soviet Union. In 1918, Soviet climatologist Wladimir Koppen defined a desert as a territory with less than 10 inches (250 mm) of precipitation annually. Water that falls as rain, snow, or hail is precipitation. Territories having between 10 and 20 inches (250 and 500 mm) of rain would be termed *steppes.* Of all the land above sea level, 14 percent is desert and another 14 percent is steppe. In total, deserts and steppes cover up to 16 million sq. miles (40 million sq. km) of this planet's 58 million sq. miles (149 million sq. km) of habitable land above sea level.

The total extent of the desert lands of Africa and Asia is astonishing. To journey from any part of the West African coast, for example from Morocco or Mauritania to the western regions of India, a person must travel through the desert. Desert conditions extend to the north and east in Asia, then across Turkmenistan as far as China, stopping within a few hundred miles (kilometers) of the Yellow Sea.

The desert presents a remarkable variety of forms and appearances. They range from immense valleys of shifting sand to vast rocky plains that seem to lack any form of life. Actually, throughout the whole desert, there are many species of animals and plants, each one perfectly adapted to the extreme conditions.

The Causes of Desert Formation

In theory, almost any area of the earth could become a desert if for a long time clouds did not form above it. Any area of the earth where rain did not fall, or fell rarely, and where the sun shone continually, would quickly become desert. It is not surprising, therefore, that deserts are most likely to be found in the subtropical zones of the Tropics of Cancer and Capricorn.

During the summer in the Northern Hemisphere, the sun shines straight down on the Tropic of Cancer, north of the equator. At this latitude, the heat of the earth's surface is at a maximum. However, assuming that there is no change in the angle of rotation of the earth on its axis, the sun will shine directly down on the Tropic of Capricorn, south of the equator, six months later. At this time, the maximum effect of the sun is at this latitude. As a result of these natural causes, most deserts form near these two subtropical latitudes.

Deserts may also form because of the variation in the atmospheric pressure (the weight of air) around the globe. These variations occur when some masses of air become warmer than others. Changes in the atmosphere are also the result of the rotation of the earth itself, which causes strong vertical and horizontal air streams.

To trace the atmospheric conditions that contribute to the formation of deserts, it is important to begin at the equator. Here, hot air masses rise and cause low-pressure areas that in turn travel outward to the north and south. In rising, these same air masses cool off and release moisture, which falls to the earth in the form of heavy rainstorms, typical of this tropical region. When the dry air masses

The diagram shows desert areas on the various continents of the world and the main causes for their formation. Most of the desert regions of the planet lie along two bands of high-pressure systems that cross the tropics. That weather system causes the land to be buffeted by dry winds that lose their moisture as they blow in either from the north or south.

Opposite: This diagram compares how heat is absorbed and released during the day and night, first in an arid region and then in a humid region.

1. In the diagram, one arrow equals 10 percent of the sun's heat. So it is clear that in an arid region, most of the sun's heat is absorbed during the day.

2. In a humid zone, clouds, dust, vegetation, and water on the ground's surface reflect the heat upwards.

3. In the desert, almost all the heat that was stored during the day is quickly lost at night.

4. In contrast, in humid regions only 50 percent of the heat that was stored in the ground is lost.

move on to the subtropical regions above and below the equator, high-pressure areas form. The hot, dry air descends to the earth's surface where it absorbs moisture, both from the lower layers of air and from the ground. Then the hot air rises again, continuing the cycle that keeps these regions in their parched condition.

The next band of weather conditions form to the north and south of the subtropical desert regions. There, low-pressure areas with their rising air masses create moist weather conditions that allow steppes and grasslands to form. Finally, at the polar regions, the air masses tend to descend again so that the climate is dominated by high pressure and drought. In reality, the earth's polar regions are also deserts, though they are deserts of ice. The little water that does fall cannot evaporate immediately, as it does in the subtropics.

The central Asian deserts were formed not only by global conditions but also by local factors. The effects that the great mountain ranges have on the condensation of humidity is one factor. Another factor is that the land may be a great distance from rain that is brought in from the ocean. As a result, it cannot benefit from that source of water.

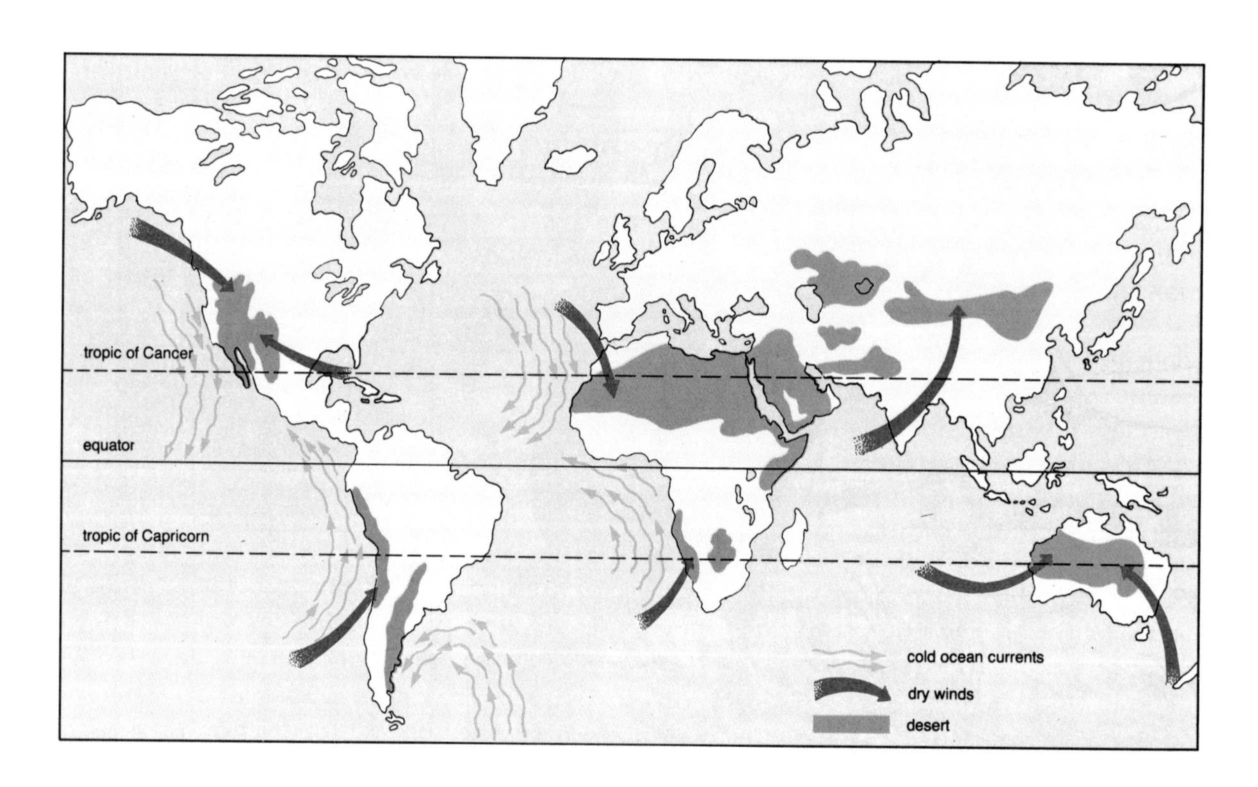

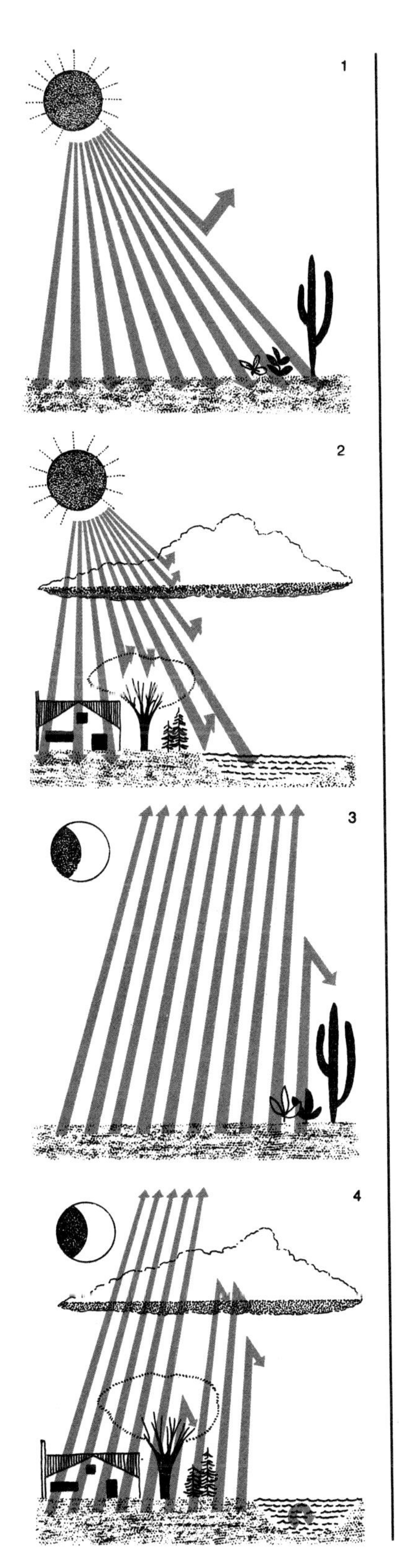

In the desert there are extreme daily changes in the weather. Because there is almost no moisture in the air, the soil is totally unprotected from the sun's rays. At night, however, the situation reverses. Up to 90 percent of the heat that was stored in the soil during the day is transferred from the soil to the atmosphere. In nondesert regions, clouds act as screens. They keep the warmth in the soil and only about half of the heat stored in the earth is lost during the night. The other half is reflected back again to the earth from the clouds and from the vegetation. In contrast, deserts undergo extremes of temperature and humidity (degree of moisture in the air). These extremes—temperatures so high that they can be fatal to plants and animals and temperatures low to the point of freezing—have dramatic effects on the living organisms.

Sometimes the wind sweeps the sand into barchans, which are crescent-shaped, moving sand dunes of the desert. Barchans may advance in a line as long as 62 miles (100 km). Depending on the force of the wind, barchans can move 100 or more feet (30 or more meters) a year and bury many large obstacles in their paths.

The Deserts of the Arabian Peninsula

The Arabian Peninsula, like an immense western door into Asia, was once the homeland of mystical Arabian horsemen. Today it is a region of modern, giant oil producers. One of the largest arid zones in the world, the Arabian Desert occupies almost the entire peninsula, covering an area of about 900,000 sq. miles (2.3 million sq. km). The peninsula is in the shape of a rectangle whose base extends from southeast to northwest for about 1,600 miles (2,575 km). The flora and fauna, or plants and animals, of the arid Arabian Plateau are so similar to those in Africa that this land seems like an isolated fragment of the African continent. Except for a few, the animals and plants of this peninsula are local varieties of forms that are widespread in Africa.

With the exception of the Hejaz coastal chain in the west and the Asir Mountains in the southwest, the entire peninsula is one of the most sterile (unproductive) areas in the world.

The Arabian Desert is made up of two great sandy areas: An Nafud to the northwest, about 28,000 sq. miles (72,500 sq. km), and Ar Rub' al Khali to the southwest, about 235,000 sq. miles (596,000 sq. km). Ar Rub' al Khali is known

A view of Ar Rub' al Khali, or "the empty quarter," the arid region that together with the Nefud region forms the great Arabian Desert. Its immense sand expanse covers a territory larger than the entire country of France. Today, it remains one of the least-explored areas of the world. Though the Arabian Peninsula is situated at the crossing point between Africa and Asia, its geographic location does not offer advantages in terms of nature. Plants and animals that grow well on one continent do not flourish on Arabian soil because the climate is not favorable. For this reason, the flora and fauna of the Arabian Peninsula are among the most sparse and limited in type of any other land in the world.

as "Ar Ramlah" by the local Bedouins, or nomads. This name means "the sands", but it implies the idea of an empty place, one so lacking in food or water that even those people who are used to the desert do not travel there. Even today it remains one of the least-explored areas on earth.

The great sandy areas are connected by two nearly parallel valleys of sand. The outer arch, Dahana, is about 775 miles (1,250 km) long and 6 to 62 miles (10 to 100 km) wide. The inner arch is shorter and has six long, sandy areas located in the lowest regions of the Najd central plain. A vast area of cliffs and low plateaus make up the rest of the plain. The largest of these areas, Nafud Ad Dahy, is located in the center and extends more than 300 miles (500 km) to the south. East of Dahana, thin strips of hammada (rocky desert) and of erg (sandy desert) extend until they rejoin Nafud in the north. Nafud, where rain rarely falls, is like a huge sea of sand.

The Najd Plain, surrounded by a great number of dry stream and river beds, appears forbidden. Scientists know that long ago, in the Quaternary period (from 2 million years ago to the present) streams that originated from the Hejaz and Asir mountains in the west ran through this region. Today these ghost-rivers are almost all invaded by sand.

The Salt Deserts

Large areas of salt, called "sebkha" in the desert regions, are common in eastern Arabia. Located on the coastal plains, the sebkhas are gently sloping sandy terraces where salt water concentrates on and below the surfaces. They are formed little by little when sand completely fills shallow bays at the seaside. Salt also forms in places where the sea level is low or decreasing and the water evaporates quickly. Then the trapped sea water becomes a strong brine, or salty solution.

The north and the northwest winds, which the Arabs call the *shamal,* blow over the salty area. They uncover the crust of salt that is just below the earth's surface. Later, the winter rains fall and new brines form. As time goes on, the tides also push the salt-laden water further inland.

The salt layer of this unique area is not quite a yard (meter) thick and it is often mixed with sand, clay, and other fine deposits. The surface may not appear to be much different from the surrounding desert. One such place is the Matti *sebkha,* the largest salt desert in the United Arab Emirates. This vast area of soft, salty mud can be dangerous because travelers often do not realize that they are on the salt marsh before they sink into it.

Further to the north, the sebkhas are covered with a thin layer of salt and sand, under which is a thick layer of soft clay. These salt marshes are found on shallow sea surfaces where algae has grown over the surface and sand and salt have covered the layer of algae. In the most eastern part of Ar Rub' al Khali, there is a vast sebkha 330 feet (100 m) above sea level, which is the highest elevation this type of marsh can reach.

Salt basins can also form in landlocked valleys. In these places, running water passes over rocks, picking up mineral and salt deposits. When this water evaporates, the minerals and salts are left. These types of inland salt flats

Salt desert is seen in Iranian territory, with a mirage phenomenon at the horizon. In the desert, reflections of a distant object may appear in a distorted form. Known as mirages, these images are caused by atmospheric conditions. These salt expanses are called *sebkha, mamlahal* or *kavirs,* depending on the language spoken by people living near them. In the dry season, the salt surface becomes so hard that motorized vehicles can drive over them. After the brief rainy season they change into vast expanses of soft, salty mud. At this time they are extremely dangerous for travelers who try to cross them.

are called "mamlahal" by the Arabs. For hundreds or even thousands of years, the desert inhabitants have obtained salt from both the sebkhas and the mamlahals.

Caspian Turkmenistan

Largely unknown even to this day, Caspian Turkmenistan is one of the greatest wonders still remaining on earth. The land is fascinating because it is so remote and difficult to reach. This immense expansc of land is located in the southwestern Soviet Union and stretches eastward from the Caspian Sea to China's borders. It also shares borders with Afghanistan and Iran.

Caspian Turkmenistan is a desolate land; at least 80 percent of the area is completely uninhabitable. Making

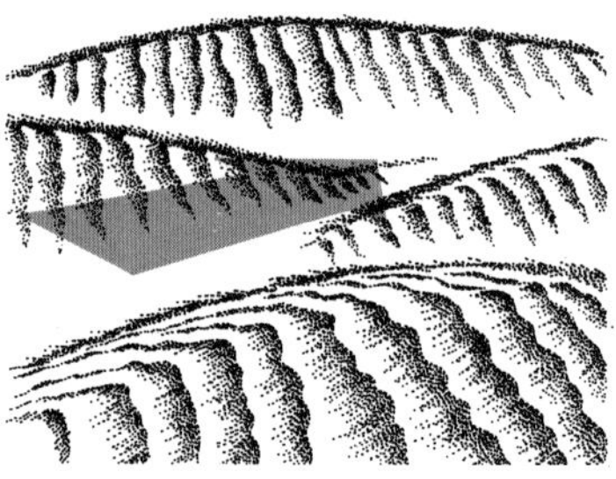

The force and direction of the wind creates different sand formations. *Above:* the half-moon shape of the barchan is due to wind blowing in one direction and in such a way that it blows the sand at the borders faster than at the center. *Upper middle:* The transversal dunes are formed by moderate winds that blow in one direction. Only the fine sand is moved. *Lower middle:* Stronger winds form the longitudinal dunes, cutting long furrows in the sand that run parallel to the direction of the wind. *Bottom:* The star-shaped dunes are formed by winds in all directions. This type of sand formation tends to remain in one place.

survival difficult are its two deserts, the Kara Kum and the Kyzyl Kum. These extend over an area so vast they are together thought of as the fourth desert of the world. The traveler who dares to venture beyond the few rivers and few inhabited areas must face sheer canyons and immense dunes that are constantly shifting with the blowing winds. At the eastern part of this territory, there are barren, towering mountains that reach higher than 20,000 feet (6,100 m).

Glaciers cover the eastern regions, known as Pamir and Tien Shan. From their icy sides, the Amu Darya and the Syr Dar'ya rivers flow down through the vast desert area and empty into the Aral Sea in the north. The area the rivers cross is so barren that the rivers are like thin lines zigzagging across a gigantic slab of marble. Though these same mountains give the desert this small amount of water, the highlands are actually the reason for the dryness of the land. When the air cools on the high peaks, the moisture that is condensed in the form of rain and snow falls on the mountains' east and south sides, away from the interior. The land exists in a state of drought and the temperatures range from extremes of 122° Fahrenheit (50° Celsius) in the shade in the summer to 5°F (-15°C) in the winter when the cold winds blow from Siberia across the Kazakhstan steppes. Life in the region must depend on the meager yearly rainfall that amounts to only 3 to 8 inches (75 to 200 millimeters). Rain comes only in late spring and early autumn.

The Kara Kum and Kyzyl Kum Deserts

The so-called black sands of Kara Kum, located in the heart of Turkmenistan, cover 72,760 sq. miles (188,500 sq. km), or three-quarters of the entire desert between the Caspian Sea and the Amu Darya River. A large part of the Kara Kum is made up of loose sands, sandy hills, and shifting dunes. The only relief is formed by the Zaunguzsk Plateau, about 200 feet (60 m) from bottom to top. The sands of Kara Kum are called "black," though in reality they don't appear to be this color at all. Below the surface of the desert there is a vast expanse of rich, black soil that is the same type the local rivers carry and deposit.

At the edge of the desert this black silt can be seen on the top of the soil. Today, the words *Kara Kum*, or "black sands," in Turkmenian, refer to parts of the desert that have some grassy cover. *Ak Kum*, or "white sands," refer to the desert where plants do not grow. *Kara* can mean "black" or "fertile." The reason behind this double meaning is clear in

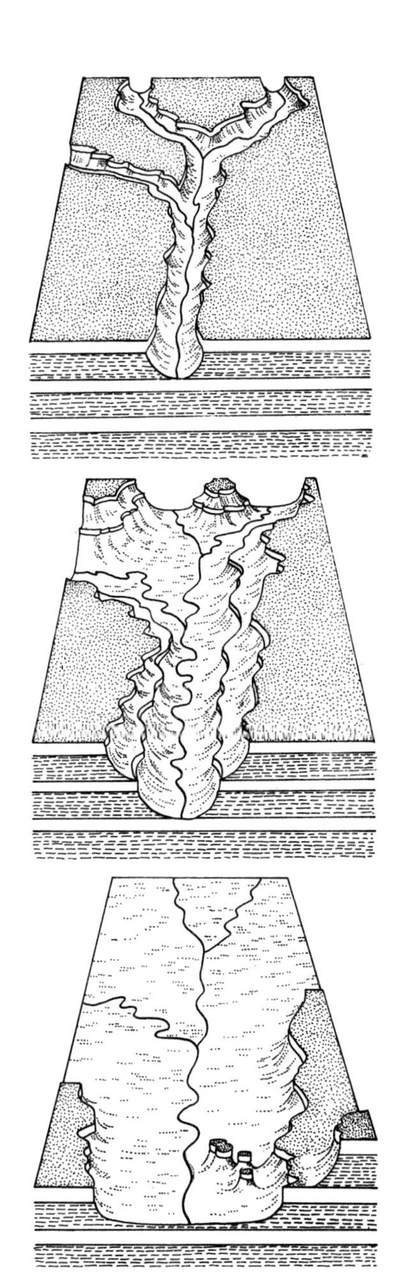

The diagram shows the erosive effects of water in an arid region. *Above:* This plateau was recently formed from a swelling of the earth's surface. At this early stage, water flows over the plateau and begins to make a deep cut in the surface. *Middle:* In later stages, deep valleys, mountains, and isolated towers are formed as the water continues to erode the land. *Bottom:* In the final stage, erosion has almost wiped out the original plateau. Almost no highlands remain and the valleys have become a desertlike plain, covered with sediment left over from the water's flow.

the spring, when brief rains soak the silt and for a few weeks areas of Kara Kum burst into spectacular bloom.

Northeast of the Kara Kum Desert is the Kyzyl Kum, which also is crossed by the Amu Darya River. A little smaller than the Kara Kum, it covers about 81,000 sq. miles (210,000 sq. km) and is known for its expanses of red sand. In fact, its name comes from the Turkmenian words *kyzyl* or "red," and *kum* or "sand." In ages past, during the Quaternary period, most of this sand was deposited from glaciers. At that time large amounts of rain and snow fell but very little evaporated, causing the rocky substrata, or land beneath the glacier, to erode quickly. The sandy deposits were left.

A typical feature of the Turkmenian deserts are takyrs. These are bare areas where the ground is like a hard clay floor that water cannot go through. Here there is no vegetation except for some lichens and algae. These deserts of clay, extending over hundreds of square miles, are formed from springs that spout up now and then inside a natural depression in the land. Muddy material builds up in those basins, and then the moisture quickly evaporates under the intense heat of the desert sun. A clay surface that becomes harder and harder over the years is left. Then strong winds blow sand over the baked earth and smooth the ground, almost as if they were polishing it. During sandstorms in this unique region, waves of sand glide over these smooth, bare takyrs as easily as if they were blowing over deserts of ice.

The barchans, or the shifting sand waves of the desert, are also found in this region. These famous arc-shaped dunes move because of the force of wind, and they travel at a speed of over 100 feet (30 m) a year. Even though they cover only 10 percent of the surface of the Kara Kum, these continuously shifting sands make permanent settlements difficult. To protect their villages, people plant trees and shrubs to block the sand dunes' movement, but this does not always work.

The Great and Small Balkans are two desolate mountainous ranges that rise at the western boundaries of the desert. The land here is composed of areas of rocks, sand, dry mud, and other rubble, along with a sparse growth of plants. The Turkomans call this region Barsakel'mes, or "the place of no return." The place is aptly named, for there is, in fact, no other desert zone where the annual temperature climbs as high.

A group of shepherds tends its herd on the Zagros Mountains in Iran. Shepherds of the southwestern Asian desert region live as nomads, or wanderers. They continuously move from place to place in search of grass for their livestock to graze on. The wild animals practice this method of survival as well. They continuously move from one region to another in search of essential water and food.

These savage lands are constantly at the mercy of various forces of nature. Earthquakes and volcanoes that spew out mud continually change the landscape, but the erosive action of the water is the most destructive. Even though the rain does not generally exceed 5 inches (130 mm) a year, the exposed surfaces are so hard and dry that even this small quantity of water may result in devastating floods that leave the land changed.

Other factors that contribute to erosion are the wind, extreme dryness of the air, and salt. Because there is such a scarcity of vegetation, the wind greatly erodes the land.

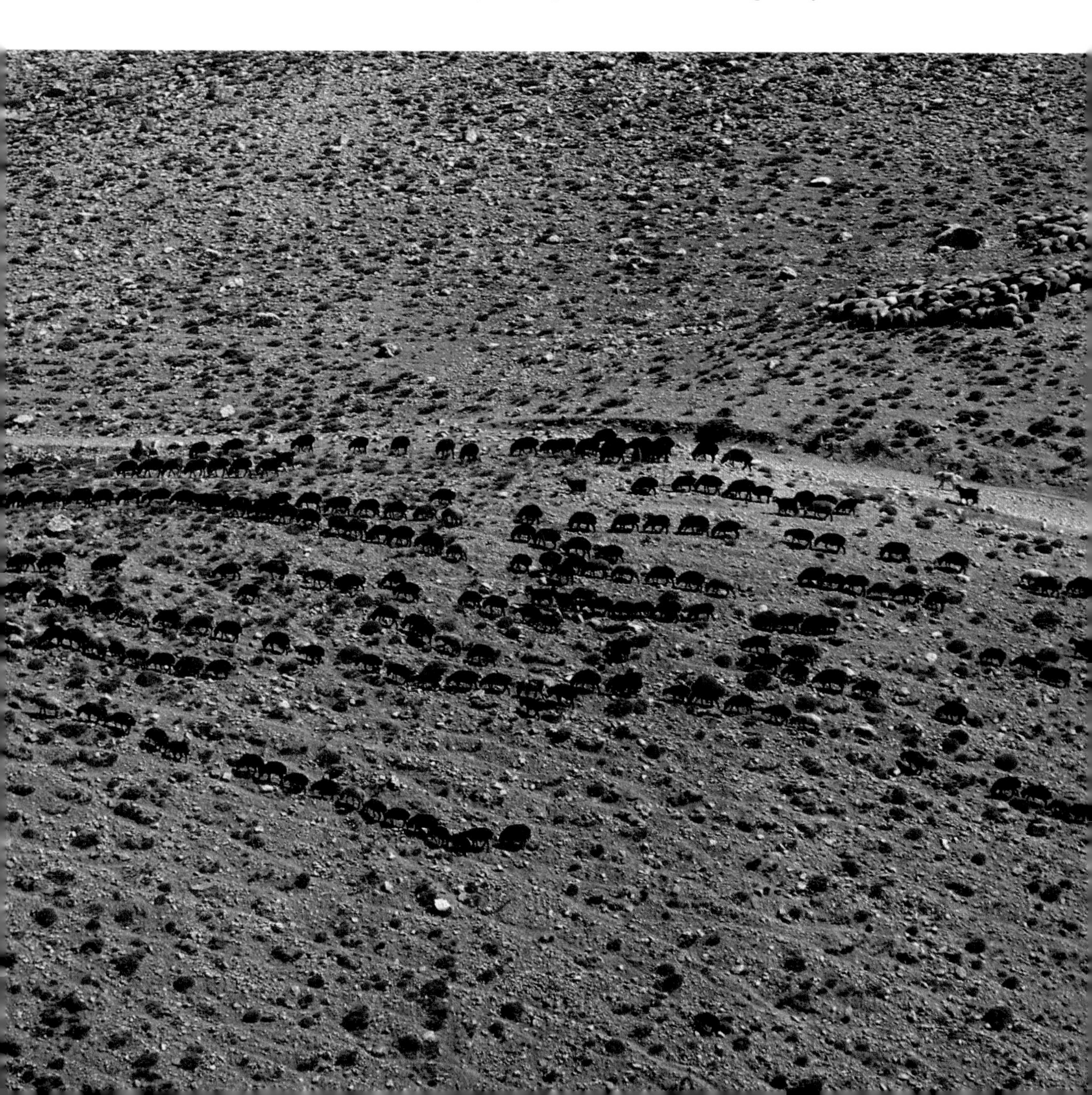

Winds in these areas blows at up to 37 miles (60 km) per hour. Carried with the force of wind is sand and clay that smooths irregular surfaces and creates sharp ridges. Here, too, salt is left on the earth after evaporation and becomes visible in the form of fine, white crystals that cover vast areas. Winds blowing off the Caspian Sea transport more salt, which adds to the white emptiness.

The earth's crust shifted long ago, creating the mountains and valleys that exist today. Caspian Turkmenistan's hot springs are actually the final effects of the changes in the earth's surface. These are known as tectonic movements, and they occurred in this region billions of years ago.

The Iranian Plateau

Bordered on the north and west by the Elburz and Zagros mountains, the Iranian Plateau is made up of three vast desert basins. These are the central plateau, the salt desert—known as kavirs—and the rocky expanses of Afghanistan and Baluchistan.

The southern portion of the Iranian Desert is one of the hottest regions of the world, with summer temperatures soaring as high as 131°(55°C). These conditions, along with strong winds and scarce and unpredictable amounts of rain, make it difficult for animal and plant life to survive.

The many salt deposits are an outstanding feature of the plateau. One of these kavirs, or undrained basins, is the Dasht-e-Kavir Desert located near the Elburz Mountains. Here the soil has a great deal of salt, which comes from the earth's phreatic strata, or the level of underground wells. In this area these are not far from the surface. The great masses of salt rest on a mud base and are crossed by deep gorges that are left after flash floods or water flow have cut through the surface. As a result, there is no way to travel overland.

According to local legends, the mythical city of Lot, which is also called Sodom in the Bible, lay in the eastern part of this territory, which is known as Kavir-e Lut. As told in the Bible, God warned Sodom's dwellers of their evil ways, but the people refused to repent. To punish them, God changed the entire area into salt, leaving it completely without life.

Finally, the region is known for occasional lone inselbergs, which are isolated hills that dot the plateau. These hills have steep slopes formed by the force of erosion.

Southward lies the Dasht-e Lut Desert, where areas of sand and stones extend from northwest to southeast for

A predesert environment is seen in transition between the steppe and the hammada, in southern Iran. The "calanque" style of erosion is visible in the background. This type of erosion, which is common in the desert regions, occurs on the rocky hills that have no trees or plants of any kind growing on them. They are completely exposed to the weather's wearing effects.

about 685 miles (1,100 km) at about 1,970 feet (600 m.) above sea level. The barchans here resemble enormous waves that rise as high as 50 feet (15 m). They seem to be frozen in a solid, endless sea of sand. At sunset, they take on breathtakingly beautiful colors.

Covering about 965 sq. miles (2,500 sq. km) the Sistan depression extends as far as Afghanistan. This depression is a bowl-shaped area of land that lies 990 to 1,150 feet (300 to 350 m) above sea level. Its lowest point is around Lake Hamun-e Saberi. Toward the end of June, the *sado-bistoruz,* which means "the wind that blows from the northwest for 122 days," begins to blow in this region. This fierce wind continues night and day, cloaking the entire area in a blanket of salt.

The sandy Rigestan Desert runs along the left bank of the Helmand River. Rising 1,640 to 4,920 feet (500 to 1,500 m) above sea level, this desert lies in a depression between the mountains and occupies about 15,440 sq. miles (40,000 sq. km). It is the most arid region of Afghanistan. Numerous dry riverbeds divide the barchans into separate mounds of sand that can reach heights of 198 feet (60 m) or more.

To the north, between the Khash and Helmand Rivers, is the Dasht-e Margow Desert, which is covered with clay and gravel. The surface of the southwest portion of this desert is somewhat different. There, most of the ground is covered with sand, and it is crossed by many dry riverbeds, takyrs, and expanses of salt.

Desert Vegetation

Water is the most important ecological factor in the desert. The availability of this precious resource determines the type of vegetation that can grow there. However, since water is scarce, the desert plants develop specific ways to adapt in order to survive periods of prolonged drought and high temperatures.

Succulents are a type of desert plant that stores water in its leaves, roots, and stems. Another type is xerophytes that have developed a number of adaptations. The surfaces of their leaves are covered with a protective coat of resin and fatty substances that reduce the amount of water that the leaves release into the air. This process in which water is lost through the membranes, or pores is called transpiration. Another adaptation that helps the plant keep its moisture is the thick down that sometimes covers the leaves. Because of this protection, the dry winds cannot

Opposite: A small, thorny tree blooms in the Iranian desert. Desert shrubs and trees have numerous spines or sharp projections to protect them against plant-eating animals, also known as herbivores. Despite the difficult environmental conditions caused by the scarcity of water and the wide temperature ranges and the soil's lack of nutrients, the number of plant species able to survive and prosper in the arid regions of the earth is surprisingly high.

Ephemeral plants are plants that last a short time. They are found in the subdesert regions, such as the one surrounding Petra in Jordan where this picture was taken. These plants have adapted to the desert conditions by completing their life cycle, from germination to reproduction, in the brief span of two months, when the rainy season comes. Later, when the rains pass, the plants die and become dry shrubs. However, a great number of seeds fall from these shrubs, waiting, possibly for years, for the next favorable season to come. Finally, when the conditions are right, these seeds can sprout once again. If the climate is particularly favorable, the plants can produce two or more generations in the course of a single year.

blow directly on the leaves' open pores. The leaves are also thick, which is another water-saving adaptation.

If the plant's leaves are small in size and in number, less water will be lost. For this reason, some trees and shrubs lose all their leaves as soon as the dry season begins. Many desert plants also have spines, thorns, or other projections that keep herbivores, or plant-eating animals, from eating them.

The deserts that are almost completely without plants are the pebble deserts, known as reg. The small amount of rain that falls there stays on the soil's surface and is rapidly lost through evaporation. However, the sandy deserts, called erg, quickly absorb and store some of the rainfall. Once that moisture is in the subsoil, it evaporates slowly. Much of the water remains underground where it can be reached by the long, deep roots of the desert plants.

Among the most typical desert trees that are nourished by this hidden resource are the acacias, which can be found growing on the bottoms of the dry riverbeds, known as wadis. Two species of *Acacia,* the *seyal* and the *tortilis,* are perfectly adapted to drawing moisture from underground channels that come down from the mountains. Eventually

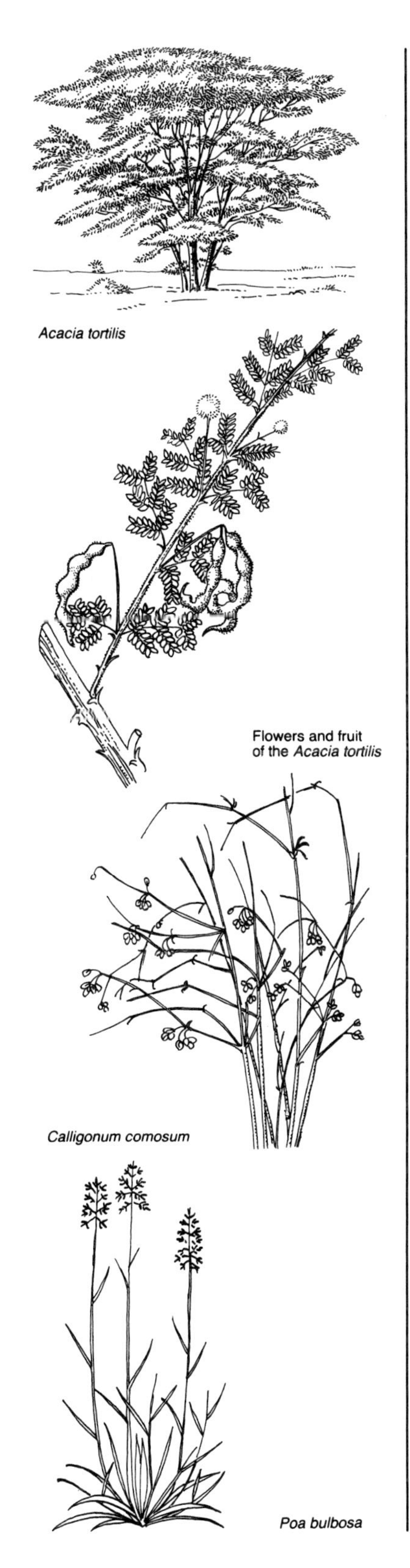
Acacia tortilis

Flowers and fruit of the *Acacia tortilis*

Calligonum comosum

Poa bulbosa

these channels trail off and dry up in the desert. Of the shrubs found in the desert, the tamarisks, with their long, deep roots, are found growing near rare springs.

The white-and-black saxual are the most common and hardiest shrubs of central Asia. The black type grows best in salty soil and has tiny, scalelike leaves. Its relative, the white saxual, thrives in sandy soil and has many small, narrow leaves.

During the hot and dry summer season, both species lose their leaves completely. Then shrubs appear to be nothing more than skeletons of dead plants. This resting period is another protective adaptation. In this state the plant loses the least amount of water to evaporation. When the rains arrive again in spring, the plant bursts forth with buds and the lifecycle begins again.

However, each season a number of branches die. The number of dead branches on the shrub increases year after year until most of the plant, and even the landscape, is covered with dead branches. The result is a strange spectacle. Vast areas of land are covered with shrubs and small trees that appear to be completely dead except for an occasional growing branch that sprouts new leaves.

Enough sunlight penetrates these strange, dense "forests"so that the living parts of trees or shrubs can be nourished. Even though most of the trunks and dry branches of these trees and shrubs are dead, they provide a helpful barrier against the wind. In an extraordinarily dry climate like that in Caspian Turkmenistan, dead saxual seldom rot and disintegrate. Instead, they accumulate and gradually become as hard as rocks.

To survive on the moving dunes, other plants have developed specialized root systems. On the sandy expanses of the Kara Kum, one of the most common plants is the three-awned grass whose buds, when they are covered by sand, produce a horizontal underground stem, called a rhizome. From this shoot, new stems grow upwards and small roots grow down. Another plant that uses this strategy is the dzhuzgan shrub which has horizontal roots that grow as long as 100 feet (30 m). Another example are the shrubs of the genus *Calligonum,* also known as sand acacias, that grow in the sandy Rigestan Desert. Though they grow only to a height of 6 feet (2 m), they have roots that may reach farther than 100 feet (30 m) from the mother plant.

Sedge are coarse grasses that are also classified as ephemerals. In spring the only vegetation that may cover some desert areas is sedge. The growth of these hardy grasses are actually helped by the herbivores that eat them. By eating the tops and tearing up the plants, the animals force the bulbous roots to split and spread. In this way, the plants push into new areas faster than plants that reproduce by means of flowers or seeds. They are therefore also adapted to deserts in which there is little rainfall. Soon after the rainy season ends, the carpet of flowering plants begins to yellow, and toward the middle of May only a few withered remains of this ingenious grass remain exposed to the sun and wind.

The drawing shows a thick group of tamarisk shrubs of the *nilotica* species, above, and the detail of a trunk with a branch partially covered by manna, below. In the book of Exodus in the Bible, manna is defined as "a fine dew, as if ground in a mortar, like hoar frost on the earth." When the Hebrews journeyed through the desert, they found this unusual substance to eat. They considered it to be a miraculous gift from God. In Hebrew, the substance is called *manhu,* meaning "what is it?" Not only did the Hebrews not understand what this welcome food was, but modern naturalists also mistakenly thought it was a secretion of the tamrisks themselves. Now scientists believe that manna is produced by some insects living on these plants. Only in arid regions can it be found in this crystalline, or solid, state. There, decomposition does not occur because the rapid evaporation of water makes the substance practically immune to bacteria.

The Tamarisk Manna

The manna of the tamarisk tree is a crystallized (hard) syrup that is described in the books of Exodus and Numbers in the Bible. Originally, people believed that the tamarisk tree, in particular the *nilotica* species of tamarisk, secreted (formed and gave off) the syrup after being overrun by an insect known as the trabutina. It is now known that manna, or "the bread of heaven" as it was called in the Bible, is a kind of honeyish, dewey substance produced by various phytophages. These are plant-eating insects, such as aphids. Others that produce this substance are psyllids, which are cicadalike insects, and white flies.

In the mountains of the Sinai, the main producer of tamarisk manna is a species of insect called *Trabutina mannipara.* On the plains of the same peninsula, the *Naiacoccus serpentinus* is the species that produces the manna. The hardened syrup, or manna, begins forming when the larvae, or very young insects, and the young female insects secrete tiny drops of a honeylike liquid. This syrup quickly dries in the dry desert atmosphere. If moisture is present in a substance, microorganisms will attack it, causing it to eventually disintegrate or rot. Manna is not subject to this type of decay, however. It is so hard, or crystallized, that no microorganisms can exist in it. As a result, manna builds up on the trees.

The Desert Locust

Many insects have succeeded in adapting to the hard conditions of the desert. Among these, the desert locust has been studied the most extensively because it has been known to do sizable damage to vegetation. The desert locust is an arthropod, or a member of a group of invertebrate animals (without backbones) with jointed legs and seg-

This immature form, or naiad, of the desert locust appears harmless. Its wings are too small to be capable of sustaining the locust in flight. However, it is possible to see that the locust is already developing an impressive chewing apparatus. Under normal conditions, locusts grow and die while remaining in what is known as the solitary phase. If their territory becomes overcrowded, the naiads gradually become more gregarious, forming large groups. Their color changes from green to brown and their wings become larger. These changes in their appearance are called morphological modifications. Even before reaching their complete development, the hopping nymphs travel in swarms, crossing over stones, small walls, or other obstacles, devouring crops and vegetation, while waiting to complete their wing growth. Then they migrate in order to continue their devastation.

mented bodies. Insects, arachnids, and crustaceans are arthropods.

Locusts are nothing more than ordinary grasshoppers that have developed the capacity to swarm and migrate. Every year swarms of these insects reproduce in hidden areas, mature, and descend on the farmlands of Asia and Africa. A single medium-sized swarm can consist of a billion locusts, each one able to consume its own weight in vegetation each day. The swarm moves without resting in its continual search for more food, often settling on more than 1,000 sq. miles (2,600 sq. km) at one time.

Locusts breed in different areas each year, depending on the amount of rain. The swarm flies downwind. As a result, the locusts are transported by the wind itself toward low-pressure areas where rain has just fallen or is about to fall. There the locusts find damp soil below the earth's surface, an ideal environment in which to hatch their eggs.

In their own effort to survive, humans often aid the invasion of locusts, though they may do this unknowingly. For example, farmers may burn dry prairie grasses or irrigate an arid zone to grow their own crops. Afterward, in

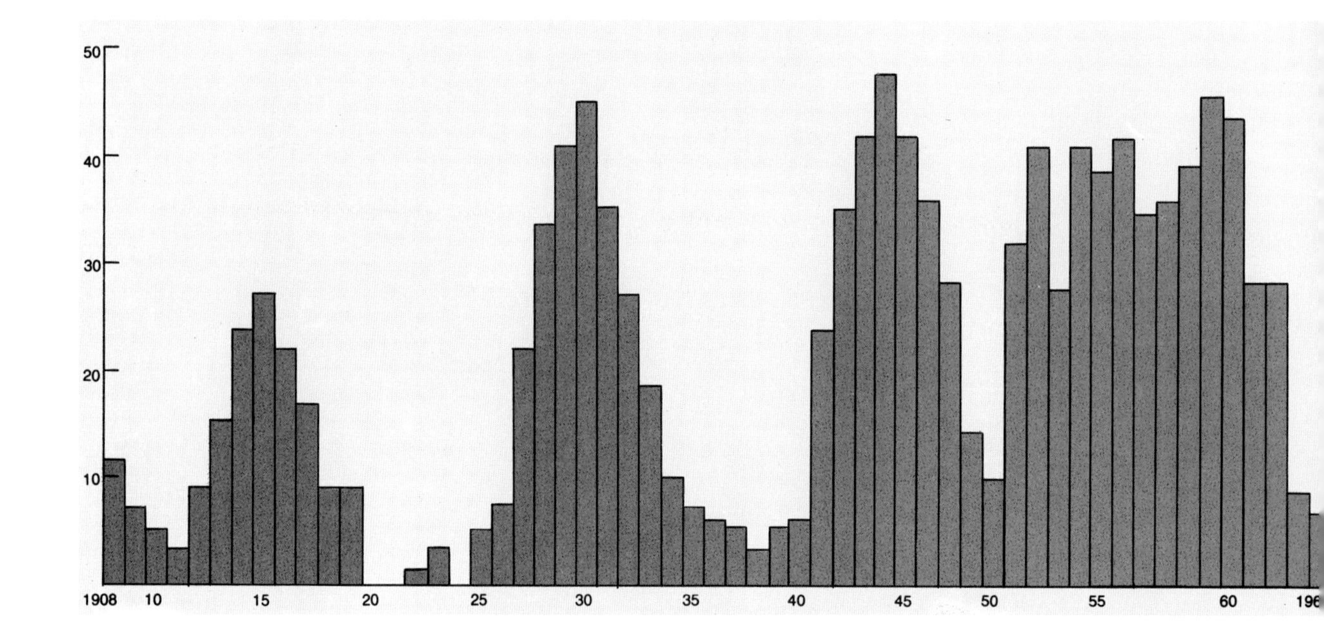

The graph illustrates the number of desert locust invasions between 1908 and 1964 in a number of territories in North Africa and in the Near East where the locust swarms have been reported. The graph shows that major invasions occur in fifteen-year cycles and that the maximum phase of the invasions lasts from five to ten years. The lined area on the map at the right shows where the locusts are born and reproduce. The dotted area indicates locations that the locusts invade. Locust invasions are a serious plague. The situation is even worse in the regions that are close to becoming deserts because these territories are already poor in vegetation, and land cultivation is difficult.

those places, many tender, new plants grow. Locusts find these perfect places to breed and grow.

The three developmental phases of the locusts are the egg, the the hopping nymph, and the flying adult. Every female lays about a hundred eggs, packed like peas in a pod.

After about fifteen days, the young are born. If they find a place in which they can survive, they exist just as other species of grasshoppers do—growing, breeding, and dying in the same place. Scientists call this the "solitary phase." However, if they find themselves in an overcrowded situation because of overbreeding, or because unfavorable weather conditions have caused a scarce food supply, the locusts move into the "gregarious phase." The locusts in this phase are long, thin, and darkly colored, in contrast to the green of the solitary phase. In the gregarious phase, locust have longer wings and tend to gather in large numbers. These insects show such remarkable differences in the two phases that, in the past, naturalists identified them as two distinct species.

In the gregarious phase, the young quickly begin to group in bands. After about a month, they develop wings, which is a sign that the locust has fully matured. At this time they begin to make brief flights, steadily consuming any suitable vegetation wherever they find it. Swarms of locusts can destroy an entire field of grain in a few minutes. The worst damage to crops and vegetation occurs in this stage, when locusts eat in large quantities to build up fat reserves.

Finally, the locust's fat presses against the stomach and pinches it. At this point, the locust stops eating and rises for its long, last flight before mating. Once in the air, the swarm flies until the locusts exhaust their energy or are driven to the ground by unfavorable conditions.

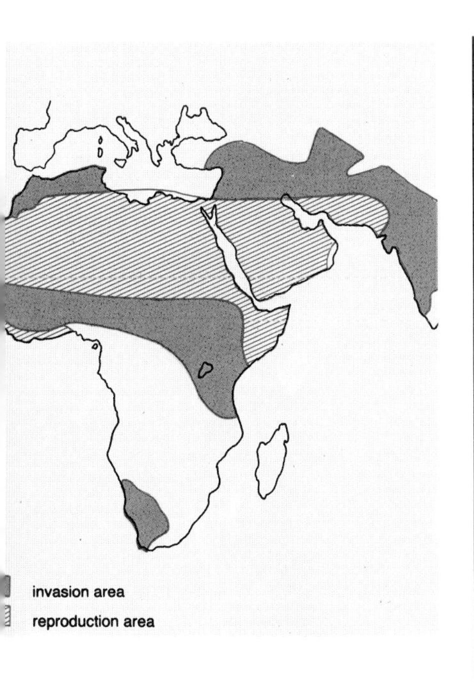

The Qanat

The possibility of permanent human settlement in the desert has always depended on the availability of water. One of the best techniques ever devised for regularly supplying water originated in Iran in 1000 B.C. This ancient system consists of a network of underground channels, called a "qanat." Because of the force of gravity, underground water sources at high levels flow into the qanat and the down to a low valley or plain. Using this system, people

This aerial view shows an Iranian village surrounded by crops in the Zagros Mountains. Due to irrigation systems, some of them ancient, water from the mountains can be carried down to the valley. Through modern technology, huge dikes have also been constructed and salt water has been made drinkable by a process called desalinization. Today farmers have learned better ways of tilling the soil so that the inhabitants are still able to cultivate these once-fertile lands. However, the soil is always in danger of becoming unproductive. In spite of these advances, only 10 percent of all Iranian land is under cultivation. Meadows, permanent pastures and woods, and simple underbrush that is often very sparse make up another 20 percent. However, the remaining 70 percent of the country's territory is totally unproductive.

can transport water to dry soil that they want to farm. Sometimes a supply of water exists near land that might be farmed, but it may be too salty. Qanats are a way of transporting fresh water where needed.

This water transport system can be found in central Iran where the plains meet the surrounding mountain chains. Here underground water can be reached at fairly shallow levels, between 66 and 330 feet (20 and 100 m) deep. The best location for obtaining the water is at the steep-sided river gorges at valley openings or in the high plains nearby. Naturalists call these gorges "alluvial cones." Once a suitable location is found, workers drill a vertical shaft until water is found, and from that point slowly dig out a slightly sloping tunnel. One benefit of this design is that there is no need for a pump. Another benefit is that there is no loss of water due to evaporation since the water is not exposed to the sun.

The upper length of the Iranian qanat has many channels that draw water from several directions and flow into a main channel. In general a qanat is only a few hundred feet or meters long, but in some places they may extend more than 15 miles (25 km). The longest qanat stretches for 100 miles (160 km).

The construction of these colossal works was accomplished in segments, beginning with the vertical shafts and then working outward on either side to build the shafts from which people can obtain the water. Normally the distance between two shafts varies from 26 to 165 feet (8 to 50 m), depending on the depth of the tunnel. All the excavated material is removed through the shafts and left around the opening. The excavated material then serves as a barrier to protect the shaft from gradually filling up with solid materials. On some qanats, covers are built over the shaft openings. From the mountains or the air, qanats are easy to spot. They appear as a line that has regularly spaced openings along either side.

Qanats are found not only in Iran, but are also in a number of arid zones from western China to the lands of the Maghreb in northwest Africa. The Spanish introduced them in South America and they still exist there today. For example, fifteen qanats are in use in the Atacama Desert in Chile. Known locally as "socavones," or mine shafts, these ducts collect water from the alluvial cones at the foot of the Andes Mountains.

Opposite: The qanat is the most ancient and still most widely used irrigation system in Iran. Qanats are slightly sloping underground tunnels that make it possible to transport water from the foot of the mountains to territories farther into the valley or the plains, where the precious resource is scarce or the springs are too salty. The craterlike depressions visible in the picture are wells that are built along the entire length of the tunnels. People can obtain water from the tunnel itself or from the wells.

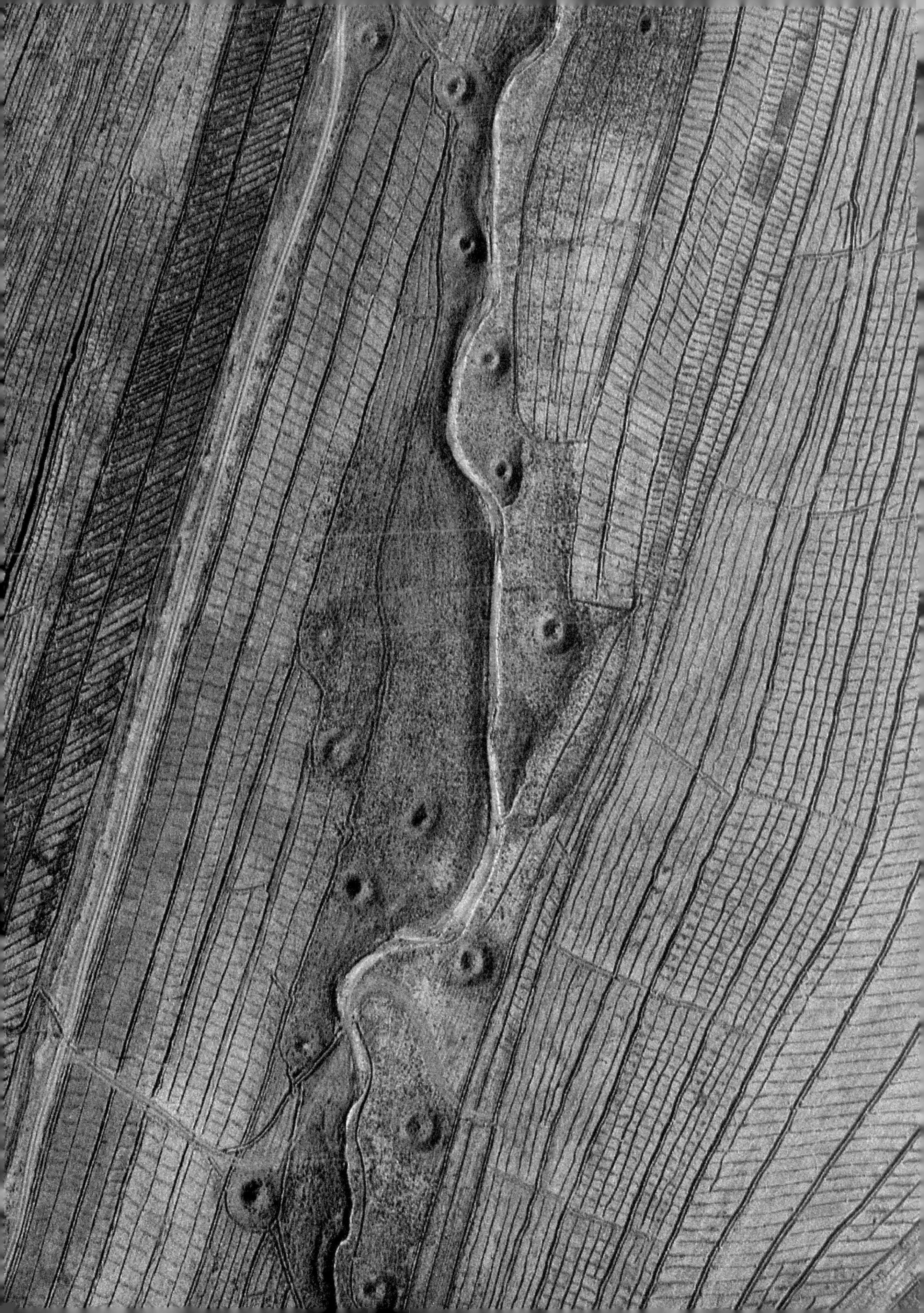

A beautiful specimen of Bactrian camel, leisurely strolls in the falling snow. The camel is not different from the dromedary merely because it has more humps; it also has a more robust frame and thicker hair. These adaptations protect the Bactrian camel in the cold climate that it inhabits. The winter temperatures in the Asian deserts drop lower than temperatures in the Sahara during the same time period.

The Bactrian Camel

The Bactrian camel is perhaps the most widely recognized symbol of the central Asian deserts. This animal still survives in the wild, unlike the dromedary, which has now disappeared outside of captivity. Naturalists agree that the few camels that do survive are genuinely wild and not descendants of domestic animals that have returned to the wild. In comparison to the domestic breeds, the wild camels have shorter brown hair and smaller humps and feet.

As recently as the middle of the nineteenth century, wild camels were still abundant in Kazakhstan and Mongolia. However, by 1920 this species could be found only in a limited area, though there were a few throughout the desert and in the dry steppes of the Gobi. Today, even in the desert regions, the wild camels, which compete with the more numerous domestic camels for food and water, have almost disappeared.

The camel family originated in North America, where fossil remains of various types of camel have been found. The smallest of these early camels were the size of a horse, while the largest reached 16.5 feet (5 m) in height at the shoulder. Today in the Americas, the camel family is found

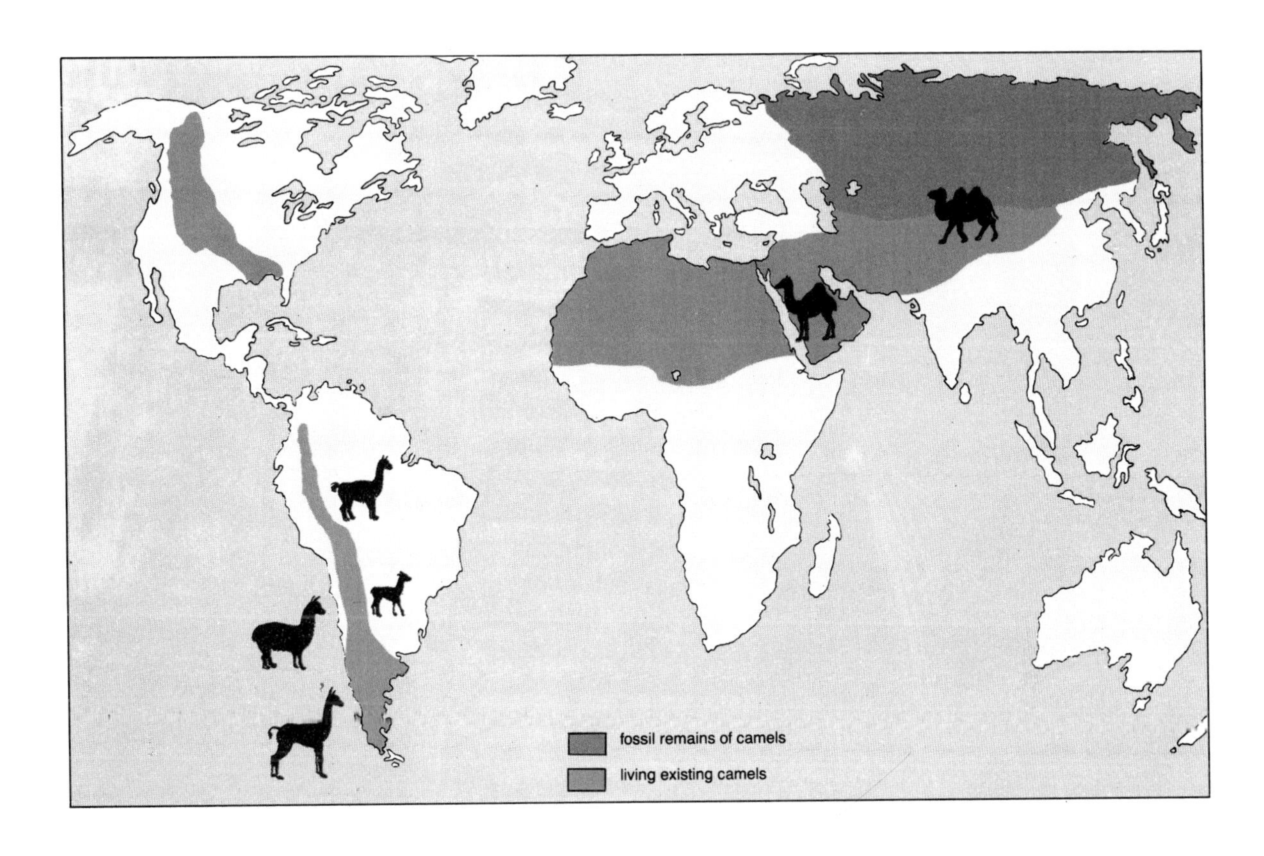

The map shows where members of the camel family are found in the world. In the Old World are the Bactrian camels which are native to central Asia, and the dromedaries, which spread from Arabia to Africa following the Arab populations. Later, camels also reached the New World through the Bering Strait. Their presence in North America, is known only by the discovery of their fossil remains. However, in South America, species of camels survive. Examples are the vicuna and the guanaco, which have no humps and have adapted to cold mountainous habitats. The llama and the alpaca are two domestic breeds that descended from the guanaco. Those two South American animals are widely used today as pack animals, or bred for their meat or wool.

only in South America and is represented by three humpless species: the llama, the alpaca, and the guanaco. Camels migrated to Asia by traveling northwest across the land bridge that once existed across the Bering Strait. In Asia this species is represented by the Bactrian camel and the dromedary.

The physical makeup of camels allows them to survive in conditions of extreme dryness. Their bodies have adapted to the desert in a particular way, for they can tolerate a loss of water up to 25 percent of their body weight. Most other mammals can tolerate a water loss of only 12 to 15 percent of their body weight. The difference is that, in the camel, water is stored in body tissues and in the intestines before it is stored in the blood. As a result, during a moderate period of dehydration, or water loss, the volume of blood remains normal and the camel's heart functions normally as well.

Camels can consume incredible quantities of water, drinking up to 30 gallons (115 liters) in one watering. The blood and tissues become hydrated (waterlogged) so quickly that, in comparison, any other mammal would die of water

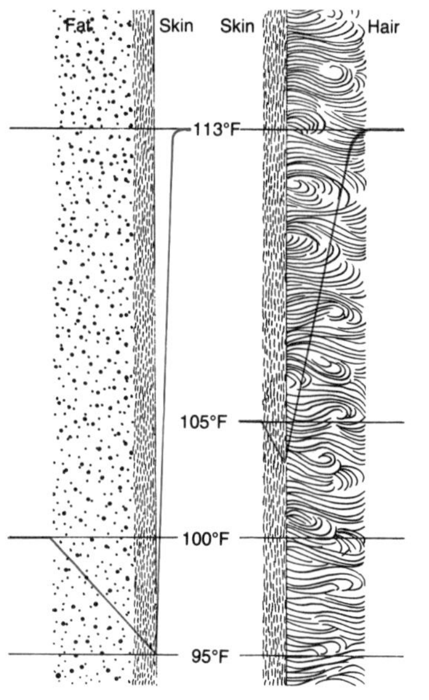

poisoning after drinking a similar amount.

The reason that the camel can take in so much water is related to its physiology, that is, the particular way that the red corpuscles function in the camel's blood. The water is absorbed by these corpuscles, or erythrocytes, which can swell to twice their initial volume without bursting. Other liquids are not as likely to reach the corpuscles and dilute the water.

Camels cannot do without water, but they adapt to arid climates because they have the ability to regulate their use of water in particular ways. Even at very high temperatures, they can limit the amount of water lost in their urine and feces, and even the amount lost from transpiration, water that evaporates from the surface of the body. Another protection is the thick hair that grows on the camel's back. This growth serves as a barrier against the sun's rays.

The old notions that camels can store water in their

Opposite, above: Dromedary camels water in northern Afghanistan.

Opposite, below: Though the desert temperature may reach 113°F (45°C), the skin surface, or epidermis, of human beings must stay at 95°F (35°C). This balance is maintained because humans perspire. However, humans lose a great deal of water in the process. In contrast, the skin surface of the dromedary is covered with thick hair (shown on the right side of the diagram) that traps a layer of air at a lower temperature. Loss of body water is greatly reduced. For this reason, the dromodary needs less water than humans in an arid environment.

Above: In their battles over females, camels try to bite the legs of their adversaries, a strategy that causes them to fall to the ground. Often, however, both animals fall, giving a male who is not in the battle the advantage.

humps and that the fat contained in the humps can be a potential water source are not true. The hump is actually stored fat. The difference between this method of storing fat and the way other mammals store their fat is that the camel's fat is stored in one place. In other mammals it is stored in a layer that lies under the entire skin surface. For the camel, this fat storage is another adaptation to its dry climate. The part of the camel's body that does not store fat can then quickly release heat, thus keeping itself cooler. In other desert species, such as the wild sheep, fat builds up in the tail or in the rump, for the same reason.

Many plant-eating ungulates, or hoofed animals, mate in the autumn and give birth the following spring. The reproductive cycle of the camel is different. Camels mate during the rainy season in February and the young are born after a gestation period (pregnancy) of around four hundred days. Before mating, the males bite and fight each other to win a particular female, sometimes inflicting serious wounds during the battle. In the course of these fights, the back of the roof of their mouths, which is the soft palate, swells up and looks like a kind of balloon coming out of the mouth. This is a signal for the battle to come to an end. The camels also use harmless ways of cowing one another, such as making low, roaring sounds or vomiting the stinking, half-digested contents of their stomachs on their opponents.

The Slaughter of the Gazelles

In the last century, great herds of gazelles of three different species—Arabian, goitered, and dorcas—could be found in the Middle Eastern deserts. They were preyed upon by the Asian lion, the cheetah, and the reddish brown desert lynx. Various races of wild asses also grazed on the vast steppes that spread from the Near East to India. Even in the heart of the deserts of the Arabian Peninsula, these large herbivores were able to find environments suited to their existence.

The legends that sprung up about the fabled unicorns were inspired by the famous Arabian oryx, a large, white antelope with long sabre-shaped horns that flourished in both the sandy and stony deserts.

The nomadic Bedouin tribes used to hunt the oryx, the ostrich, and the houbara bustard for food. Their hunting never threatened the populations of these animals with extinction, however. The rapid and tragic decline of these species began later, after the discovery of oil. The profits

Dorcas gazelles, pictured here, are among the most graceful animals of the Asian deserts. The genus *Gazella* includes about fifty species, the majority of which are dispersed throughout Africa. In all of Asia only five species exist, all of them ranging throughout a wide territory that stretches from Palestine to India. Among these Asian species are the Dorcas gazelles, elegant little animals that weigh between 33 and 40 pounds (15 and 18 kg). Today, they are found less and less in Arabian territory since humans have begun to move into their natural habitats.

from the sale of oil brought a sudden and unexpected wealth to all the countries of the Persian Gulf. With the wealth came native inhabitants and foreigners who began to exploit the natural resources, apparently unaware of the harm that they could do to the environment.

Equipped with guns and motor vehicles that could travel cross-country over difficult terrain, these people pushed into the most remote areas of the desert. They began to dig wells in search of water and to build semipermanent settlements. This fatal combination of factors caused a serious decline of the oryx, ostriches, gazelles, and other desert animals. In some cases, species became extinct.

At the beginning of the 1950s, naturalists still believed it would be impossible that the number of gazelles would decline to the point of becoming an endangered species. In those years however, hunting groups were organized daily, resulting in the senseless massacre of 300 or more animals at a time. In some cases, hunters in as many as 100 cross-country motor vehicles lined up and proceeded to sweep across the desert, massacring any living creature they found

A splendid white antelope, with its two characteristic long slender horns. The Arabian oryx, a member of the antelope family, was once found everywhere in the peninsula. Later it almost became extinct because of excessive hunting. About sixty specimens, bred in captivity and introduced in captivity and then reintroduced in their original habitats, survive today in two nature reserves of Jordan and Oman. In 1982 two oryxes were born in the wild, an indication that this attempt to reintroduce the species is having some success. Naturalists who participated in this effort hoped to remedy the situation that was created when Arab and European oil producers hunted this species to the point of extinction.

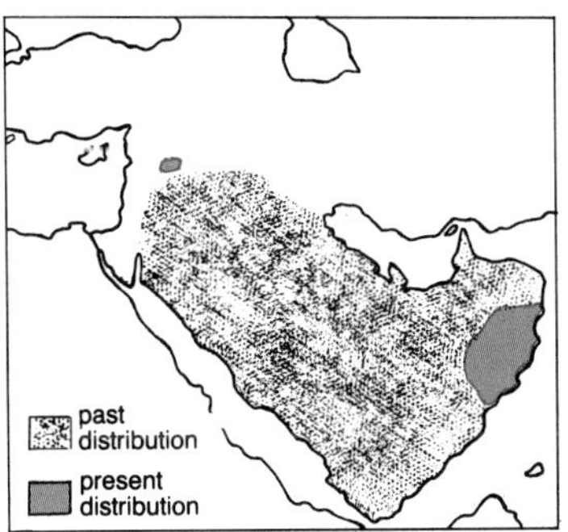

in their way. At that time, oil companies would hire crews whose job it was to scour the desert, looking for gazelles to be used as food for their workers. The hunters would use machine guns to bring down their prey.

Since this senseless slaughter, gazelles survive only in the most remote areas, on harsh, rocky grounds impossible for even the toughest cross-country vehicles to reach. Unfortunately, these are not the most favorable habitats for the few surviving animals.

The Fabled Arabian Oryx

The best-known animal of the Arabian Desert is the fabled Arabian oryx that lives on the rocky plains that border the sandy regions. In the Ar Rub' al Khali Desert, this animal is able to survive up to 186 miles (300 km) away from known springs. It feeds on whatever few sparse shrubs and meager grasses it finds. At one time the skill of the Bedouin desert hunters was measured by the number of oryx each was able to kill. In the field the oryx can become difficult to bring down. Once trapped by a hunter, the oryx boldly attacks its enemy by lowering its long horns and thrusting and slashing with sicklelike movements. At the same time it snorts loudly and fiercely to frighten the enemy.

In the past the oryx used to roam as far north as the Syrian Desert. Then, little by little, the area it occupied was reduced to the sandy portions of the An Nafud and Ar Rub' al Khali Deserts. Even in those remote areas, the relentless massacre by hunters did not stop. The few remaining animals were even gunned down from the sky, with hunters shooting at them from small airplanes and helicopters. Because of these practices, the Arabian oryx has become extinct in its homeland. However, it survives in captivity in California's San Diego Zoo, which operates a reproduction center for endangered species. In a fortunate turn of events, oryx born in that United States zoo were taken to Oman in Arabia in the early 1980s, where the species was reintroduced into the wild.

Of all the mammals, the oryx is a truly exceptional species because of its ability to survive for long periods at temperatures as high as 113°F (45°C). Most animals would die in a temperature of 108°F (42°C). The oryx has an adaptive mechanism that protects it in such high temperatures. Under its brain is a small network of blood vessels that are somewhat cooled when the animal pants. The blood that passes from these blood vessels to the brain is never

higher than 108°F (42°C). In this way the sensitive brain tissues are protected from the scorching temperatures in the Ar Rub' al Khali Desert.

The Ostrich

The ostrich is typical of the Arabian Peninsula. It is also found in the arid and semiarid zones of Africa south of the Sahara. Just as the camel is the best adapted of all the large mammals to live in the desert, the ostrich is the most suited for the desert of all the land birds. To survive in the desert, the ostrich has developed special behaviors that help it retain water.

The ostrich has long feathers thinly covering its back. When exposed to high temperatures, the bird deliberately raises these feathers so the sun's rays are kept farther away from the bird's skin. Underneath the feathers, heat is quickly released through the skin. The slightest breeze can speed up this cooling process considerably. However, when the air temperature is higher than its body temperature, the ostrich must pant in order to keep cool.

Above: Ostriches flee, probably frightened by the photographer's vehicle. At the beginning of the twentieth century, the ostrich was widespread in Arabia and also in Syria, Iran, and Turkestan. By 1914, however, it was found only on the Arabian Peninsula and since 1941 this bird has not been seen even in these territories. Ostriches survive in the wild only on the African continent. To increase their numbers, a program has been underway in Israel for some time in which ostriches are bred in special enclosures. Once mature, they are reintroduced into their native habitats.

Opposite page: The female ostrich performs an intricate dance as part of the mating ritual.

Ostriches, like all birds, have two balloonlike extensions of the lungs, or air sacks, that are part of the cooling process. Even the corneas of the eyes have a role in cooling. When the bird inhales dry air, water evaporates from the damp, mucous membranes of the nose, cooling it. When the bird exhales, the now warm, moist air from the lungs passes over the cooled mucous membranes, where it condenses and creates humidity again. At night, when the air temperature decreases, the ostrich flattens its feathers so that they snugly cover the body. In this way a layer of warm, insulating air is trapped to protect the bird during the cold night.

The ostriches are definitely gregarious animals that always live in groups. In fact, they do not limit themselves to forming groups among their own kind. They also join herds of antelope, a habit that has certain benefits for both species. Because the ostrich sees at a level about 9 feet (3 m) above the ground, the sharp eyes of these large birds detect the presence of predators sooner than the antelope. On the other hand, the antelope's sense of smell allows them to detect enemies that are hidden from the ostriches' vision.

THE STEPPES OF WESTERN ASIA

After the desert, the grasslands are the most common type of terrain in Eurasia. Few trees grow in this vast steppe. It extends from the treeless Hungarian plain, or puszte, through the Ukraine and the entire length of the southern Soviet Union. It finally ends in Altai in Mongolia. With its slightly rolling, open terrain and few mountain barriers, the steppe has always been the chosen route to travel between the east and west.

Immense Expanses of Grass

Compared to the deserts, the climate of the steppe region is nearly as hot in summer, but colder in winter. Much more rain falls on the steppe than on the desert, so grasses grow abundantly there. Because of this vegetation, the topsoil is very fertile and tends not to erode.

These immense expanses of grass have remained practically untouched by humans until recent times. In the last century, however, the plains have been greatly changed by farming. Today only small sections of the original steppe remain, almost all of them in national parks and nature reserves. The last steppes converted to farmlands were in the driest area. In recent times modern methods of irrigation have been applied to these very inhospitable lands. Only certain grasses are able to survive in these semidesert areas where the rainfall is only slightly more than in the actual desert.

The origin of the Eurasian steppes can be traced to the end of the last glacier age (about 10,000 years ago). The ice masses left deposits of soil laden with sand and clay. During that period most of Europe was a great steppe whose grasses grew on a base of silt, rock fragments, and debris deposited by the melting ice. Naturalists have learned from the fossil remains found in the region that great herds of wild horses, saiga antelope, European bison, and other herbivores lived on these great expanses of grass.

The open land gave way to forest when the climate grew warmer. Throughout most of Europe, the trees overtook the steppe. However, in the far eastern regions of Europe, the great expanse of grass and bulbous plants, as well as the wildlife on this terrain, stayed intact.

Opposite: This desolate-looking steppe is found on the border between Iran and Afghanistan. The steppe is less desolate than the desert but occupies an equally large amount of land in the heart of Asia. In the past, travelers who were going on foot to the East crossed this terrain.

The Flora

Grasses dominate the plant life of the steppe. Most of them belong to the Graminaceae family, which covers the Eurasian steppe and grasslands elsewhere. They are plants

with long, straight stems that are often hollow. The stems tend to swell at the points where the leaves are attached.

Many of these grasses also produce horizontal, rootlike stems from which new shoots grow. When this type of root grows underneath the soil, it is called a "rhizome." When it creeps above the ground, it is called a "stolon."

The grasses are ideally suited to survive even if rainfall is irregular or if plant-eating animals graze on them. Like many other plants, new growth occurs at the plant's base, not at the tip. So when a grazing animal eats the upper stem and leaves, the grass regrows quickly. In fact, grazing and frequent cutting are a natural way to stimulate the production of new stalks. Meadows thicken for this very reason.

Among the most common grasses of the Eurasian steppe are sheep's fescue, stipa grass, the species of grass known as *Koeleria pyramidata,* crested wheatgrass, and, toward the end of the summer, the involute-leaved sedge. This grass is a coarse type that grows in clumps and has leaves that roll inward at the edges. Such flowers as daisies and kochias grow among the grass in some areas.

Many other blooming plants appear when the spring rains fall on the grasslands. Among them are the red and yellow tulips, yellow or blue-violet dwarf iris, and dark red, fringed peonies. Occasionally, clumps of nodding sage with beautiful blue flowers can be found. Colchicum, crocus, and grape hyacinth grow in the southern regions of the steppe.

Small shrubs also grow in some areas, especially where the ground is slightly hilly. In these locations, the dwarf almond trees, broom, and spirea grow.

At the other extreme, where the steppe meets the desert, a mixture of the two environments exists at the area near the border. There are fewer areas covered by the grassy carpet. In its place are patches of rocky, sandy ground where tufts of sparse grass grow.

As the dark, humus-rich soil of the steppe gives way to the brown soil of the semidesert, the vegetation begins to change little by little. The mugworts and wormwoods, known for their aromatic (pleasant) scents, are some of the most typical and abundant plants found in the semidesert. Two species of grass that dominate the region are the wormseed, which grows in sandy soils, and a grass of the *Artemisia pauciflora* species, which thrives in the salty desert soil.

In the dry seasons, the leaves of these plants are curled, which is a natural way of reducing water loss. At this time, they seem to be completely withered and dead. However, with the first spring rains, the blackish, scorched branches sprout buds that quickly grow into tall stalks. Clusters of grayish flowers adorn the stalks. These tiny flowers that grow together on a single stem are called "inflorescences."

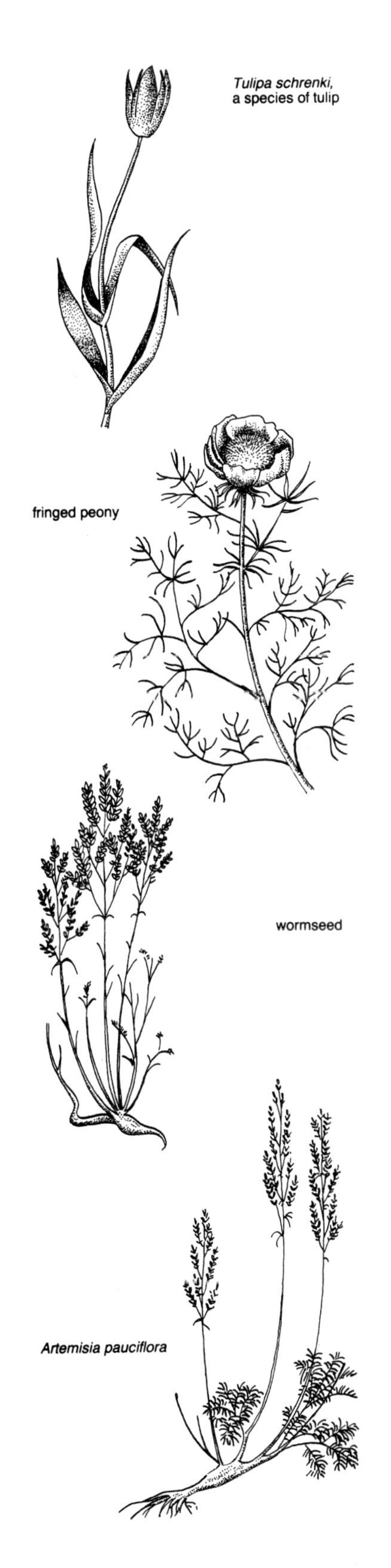

The Great Herbivores

Animals that live in the steppe have developed special ways to adapt to their environment, just as animals in the desert have adapted to their hot climate. On the open stretches of grass, the scorching summer sun is difficult to avoid, and the moisture in the air can vary widely. In the daytime the humidity can be very low, while at night it rises to high levels. These animals of the steppe do not migrate to warmer climates in winter. They stay on the open grassland where there is almost no protection from the cold winds that sweep continuously across the great treeless expanse.

The survival of large grazing animals living in the steppe and the semidesert depends on their ability to move continuously over the large areas of land. They flee the intense cold and snow and search for pastures. The animals that tend to group together and form large herds are better able to survive in this unpredictable environment as they search for new sources of food. Where the rains fall in a regular seasonal pattern, these wanderings follow a regular route. However, if the rains fall only now and then, the animals are forced into a ceaseless nomadic existence. During prolonged droughts or period of intense cold, the animals may die off in large numbers.

Przewalski's Horse

Of all the plant-eating animals of the steppe, the most typical is the Przewalski's horse. Though it has almost disappeared today, it remains the only authentic wild horse still living. Generally these "wild horses," including those found in the western United States, are just domestic animals or their descendants that have returned to live in the wild.

A colonel of the czar army, Nikolai Przewalski, first described this species in 1881 after finding several herds in Mongolia. In appearance the wild Przewalski's horse was larger and had a shorter mane than its domestic counterpart. It is known that this species roamed throughout most of Asia and Europe a few thousand years ago. Cave paintings of this horse show that it existed in prehistoric times.

An existing example is the Lascaux cave in France. Its dwellers in the Pleistocene epoch (from 2 million to 10,000 years ago) had drawn these horses, clearly showing the basic characteristics of wild horses: their massive heads, manes with short, stiff hairs like those on a brush, and a large body.

For early people, however, this fascinating four-footed animal, or quadruped, was a possible food source. To capture these animals, the hunters would track them in the steppe, launch a surprise attack, and drive them toward a cliff. The herd would stampede and run over the edge, and the hunters would succeed in killing a whole herd at once.

Przewalski's wild horses graze on a prairie in the Soviet Union. Ancestor of all domestic horses, this species was almost totally extinct at the beginning of this century. Today the surviving specimens have been carefully protected and these horses have begun to repopulate small areas of the Asian and European territories that they occupied in ancient times.

At the time of its discovery a hundred years ago, the habitat of the wild horse was already limited to the heart of Asia. This took in the Dzungaria in the south and west and the Gobi Altai in the northeast. These regions did not offer many ideal habitats for Przewalski's horse. The species stayed there only because the Dzungaria and the Gobi Altai were places where they were somewhat safe from the nomads who hunted them for their meat and hide. Furthermore, they did not have to compete with the herds of domestic horses for food and water. These regions represented a kind of last refuge.

Nomads moving into these remote areas probably caused the extinction of the wild horse in its natural habitat. This animal was then forced to migrate in the heat of midsummer to the most desolate and desertlike regions. There it survived probably by finding the most remote oases and feeding on shrubs soaked with salt, tamarisks, mugworts, wormwoods, and grasses. In captivity, however, a few wild horse specimens have survived. Between 1889 and 1901, the first attempt to take the Przewalski's horses from the wild and protect them in captivity resulted in the capture of about fifty. However, the entire population living today in zoos is descended from only eleven stallions and one mare caught in 1947.

As early as 1906, efforts were underway to breed these horses in captivity. Scientists crossed a Przewalski's stallion with a domestic mare. The offspring born from this union were in turn used in a program to breed wild horses in captivity. The scientists realized that more Przewalski's horses would be needed to prevent interbreeding and to enrich the genetic pool.

Now about 350 survive in captivity. The fact that these few specimens remain represents the only chance that the little horse of the Mongolian steppes may soon return to populate its former home in Asia.

The Wild Ass

The fastest and most robust member of the Equidae family, or horse family, was undoubtedly the Asiatic wild ass. This was found in great numbers, ranging over a number of territories, from western Asia to Mongolia. Today it is threatened with extinction.

An important subspecies is the Syrian wild ass, which is also in danger of extinction. This wild ass once roamed throughout the Syrian Desert, Arabia, and Iraq, but it has not

The table shows three distinct subspecies of the Asiatic wild ass. *From left to right:* The kiang, native to the Tibetan plateau; the dzeggetail, once widespread throughout eastern Europe, but present today in only a few areas of Mongolia; the onager, still surviving in only a few areas of Iran, the Soviet Union, Afghanistan, and in some arid territories of northern India.

been sighted since 1927. The Syrian wild ass differs in appearance from the wild horses in that it has longer ears, a straight-backed, short body, and a tail that ends in a tuft of hairs.

Another subspecies of the ass has survived. The onager, once abundant in Iran and in the southernmost areas of the Soviet Union, survives today on the salty steppes of northern Iran and the neighboring regions of the Soviet Union.

Finally, a third subspecies is the kulan of central Asia, which was common on the Kirghiz steppes and in Mongolia. Like Przewalski's horse, this animal was forced to abandon its natural habitat because nomadic shepherds moved into the most remote areas of the steppe. Though it can run up to 45 miles (75 km) per hour, its speed was not enough to escape the hunters who drove cross-country vehicles.

Wild asses have long been hunted for their meat and hides and have also been widely used as beasts of burden. Before horses were imported to Mesopotamia, the people used wild asses to pull all their vehicles. Hunting these animals was also one of the favorite sports of Persian nobles in ancient times.

Today the wild ass is protected in the Badkhyz Reserve,

This Asiatic wild ass has had its tail damaged. Males of this species have strong territorial behavior and often battle with each other to defend their own harem. Therefore it is normal to find specimens with scars or with tails somewhat cropped. Because this animal is so fierce, the wild ass has been practically impossible to domesticate. Domestic asses are actually descended from much tamer, wild African specimens.

which was founded in 1941 for just this purpose. In 1953 a stallion and seven mares were transferred from Badkhyz to the island of Barsakel'mes, a reserve in the Aral Lake. The first attempt failed because the stallion turned out to be impotent (unable to make a female pregnant). Two years later, it was replaced by a second specimen. This time the mares did give birth, the first occurring in 1957. Since then the ass population of Barsakel'mes has rapidly increased.

Wild asses live in groups of six to ten, each led by a mature stallion. When threatened by a predator, the stallion places itself between the herd and the aggressor so the mares and foals can be the first to flee. In autumn the small groups of asses become nomadic as they search for food.

The breeding season starts at the beginning of summer, when the stallions engage in heated battles over the females. After the stallion and mare mate, the pregnant female has a gestation period of eleven or twelve months. At the end of that time, the mare gives birth to a single foal. This newborn is usually able to walk within a few hours, but stays hidden in the tall grass for the first week of its life. After that brief time it runs and follows its herd. At one month of

Above: A section of the saiga's snout shows how the shape of the proboscis is the result of an enlarged nasal cavity. This empty space functions as a place where cold winter air is heated before entering the lungs of the antelope.

Below: Two female saiga antelope graze.

age the foal is already able to feed itself to some extent by grazing. However, for the first year of its life the foal is nourished by its mother's milk.

The Saiga Antelope

The saiga antelope represents the best example of an herbivore, or plant-eating mammal, that has adapted to the harsh climate of the Eurasian steppes. It has accomplished this by developing a pattern of migration.

Saiga antelope live in immense herds that often number up to 100,000 individuals. Because they are exceptionally mobile, they increase their chances of escaping the most violent winter storms by moving on to seek areas where the snow covering is not so deep and food can be reached. In the same way, the herds leave the areas of drought in the summer and migrate great distances to find new sources of food and water.

Once the saiga was scattered throughout the entire arid and grassy steppes of the Asian continent, from the most western regions of the Soviet Union to eastern Asia. By 1920, however, overhunting had almost reduced it to extinction. This antelope became even more sought-after when it was thought that its horns had medicinal (healing) properties. Human hunters and animal predators, such as wolves,

When saiga females are about to give birth, they move to the most desolate and remote territories of the steppe, so that the defenseless offspring do not have to fear the attack of predators. In these regions, the calves are also harder to spot because they are perfectly camouflaged among the little mounds of earth raised by the wind or by the digging of rodents.

pursued it for its meat. Finally, the entire population of saiga antelope was greatly reduced from many millions of individuals to a few hundred. The species would have certainly become extinct if the Soviet Union had not made the hunting of these antelope illegal and began a program to create a habitat that would encourage the animals to increase.

Today the saiga is particularly abundant in Kazakhstan, where an estimated two million survive. They have once again become a true natural resource. In addition, they are now a source of profit since the government has made it legal to slaughter about 300,000 yearly.

One factor that contributed to the rapid recovery of the saiga is early sexual maturity of females. When only ten months old, the female can become pregnant with a single offspring. At this time, it is still a year before the female's body will be fully grown. At full maturity the pregnant female will produce two young.

The mating season occurs during November when the sexually mature males, that is males over twenty months old, try to form harems (groups of females associated with one male). These consist of up to twenty females in some cases. At this time the males are so busy fighting off rivals and mating with the females that they have almost no time to graze. Consequently, they become weak. They then attract the attention of predators, especially wolves. As a result, the majority of females become "widowed" early. After a particularly hard winter, the number of adult males that survive may amount to only 5 to 10 percent of the original number.

Generally females give birth in the most remote parts of the upper steppe, in order to hide from wolves. Here the light-colored young camouflage themselves in the sand.

One of the most remarkable characteristics of the saiga antelope is its prominent, bulbous snout. This enlargement is more developed in the male, whose snout looks short and swollen. This characteristic is especially noticeable before the mating season, and so it is believed that it may function in some way in the courtship display. Naturalists still do not agree on what purpose the swollen snout serves. It is agreed, however, that it probably is an adaptation to the high summer temperatures. The broad surface of the nasal passages are thought to help cool the blood that flows to the brain. According to one theory, the snout works as a filter to keep out dust raised by the herds as they move continuously.

Native to India, this five-striped squirrel is common even farther west, as far as eastern Iran. This animal is one type of Asiatic striped palm squirrel.

The Afghan mole lemming is a small rodent of the Asian steppes that generally chooses the subsoil as its habitat. This mole shows particular molelike adaptations, such as a pointed snout, tiny eyes and ears, and very strong legs that are structured to dig the complicated systems of tunnels in which it lives.

Rodents

Few trees and rocks are found in the Eurasian steppe to protect animals from natural enemies and from the extreme temperatures. In such a terrain, some animals live underground. Of the animals that choose this habitat, the best known are the rodents. Thousands of them may live in a single colony.

The underground homes, or burrows, have multiple uses for most of these rodents. They serve as a refuge from predators and a safe place in which to give birth. During the extreme heat of summer, a rodent may use the shelter to estivate, or fall into a semiconscious state until conditions improve. During the winter the animal may hibernate in the burrow. These animals return to the surface of the land to seek their food, feeding on the green parts and seeds of grass. They also eat the roots by skillfully extracting them from the ground.

The suslik, a ground squirrel found on most of the grassy Eurasian plains, is one of the most commonly found rodents on this steppe. Although this little animal groups in large colonies, every individual occupies its own burrow. This underground dwelling consists of a main entrance tunnel about 20 feet (6 m) long and numerous side corridors. The nest for the young, in the female's tunnel, can be found as deep as 6.6 feet (2 m).

Some species of rodents, especially the mole lemmings, zokors, and mole rats, live completely underground. To the average observer, they resemble moles. Their eyes are very small or even covered with a layer of skin. The larger mole rat, which digs burrows at a fast rate, using its head as a bore, can do so because its eyes and ears have atrophied, or become useless.

These strange rodents dig underground tunnels as deep as 16.5 feet (5 m). They accumulate large quantities of food for winter and store them in various side rooms. They are solitary animals who avoid the other individuals of their species, except when males and females associate during the brief mating period. In fact, if the male does not leave the female immediately after mating, she chases him in a violent attack.

Like other burrowing rodents, the bobak marmot affects the surface soil by its constant digging. As a result, the makeup of the soil and the grassy layer is constantly changing. Each animal carries large quantities of subsoil to the surface, and carries back grass and other organic material to be used as nest litter. The rodents also deposit excrement in specially constructed "dead-ended" sections of the burrow. The material that the rodent brings in or deposits underground quickly changes into humus. After several years, the soil enriched with the rodent's leavings can become exceptionally deep. It was this type of composition that made up the famous *chcrnozen* soil, which was the original soil of the fertile steppe.

The tunnels of the bobak marmot are even longer and deeper than those of the mole rat. A single marmot digs up to 200 feet (60 m) of passages, all of which open to the nesting room. Mounds of soil rising as high as 49.5 feet (15 m) pile up around the opening of the burrow. Underground, ten to fifteen marmots share a burrow that may be composed of hundreds of tunnels.

The number of several species of rodent is increasing, partially as the result of increased human activity on the steppe. Herdsmen have brought in their cattle, sheep, and goats, which often overgraze, killing off the original grasses. The surface vegetation then changes from edible grasses to types of low underbrush that do not make good grazing for domestic animals. However, this new growth becomes a perfect habitat for rodents.

One species that has increased since the turn of the century is the five-toed jerboa, the largest of all jerboas. The rear legs of the jerboa are four times longer than the front. The animal generally moves in little jumps, using all four limbs. When frightened, it makes huge leaps using its rear legs only. The jerboa may cover over 10 feet (3 m) in one of these long jumps. This bipedal motion resembles the two-legged movement of the kangaroo and some Australian desert lizards. It is a protective adaptation for animals who must move fast on an open terrain. The long rear legs also keep the animal some distance above the scorching desert soil. The short front legs are used for digging and drinking. Finally, the long tail is an adaptation that helps the jerboa keep its balance during long jumps.

When the jerboa is exposed to temperatures above 104°F (40°C), it secretes large quantities of saliva to help lower its body temperature. Most often this animal stays in the cooler underground burrow during the day in order to conserve energy and water. The jerboa's ability to conserve water is truly exceptional. It is capable of surviving indefinitely on a diet consisting only of dry seeds, until water is available.

Opposite: Some of the most typical rodents of the Asian steppe are pictured here. Circling over them is a long-legged buzzard, a dreaded predator. *Top, from left to right:* A bobac marmot in its characteristic lookout position on top of the earth mound that opens to its den; a golden hamster, which emerges from the subsoil exclusively at night; two specimens of suslik, typical ground squirrels with a spotted coat; a jerboa with its large ears and long legs adapted to jumping, also a nocturnal animal; another bobac marmot, asleep inside its den; and finally, a greater mole rat, a unique, practically blind rodent which, like moles, lives by digging tunnels and feeding on roots.

The European polecat is a small and very well-known carnivore. It lives in the woods and fields of most of temperate Eurasia. It is attracted to human-made structures, and will sneak into houses, haylofts, or wood piles. Between April and May it finds a well-hidden spot where it produces from three to eleven young. Two other polecats can be found in eastern Europe: the marbled polecat, whose territory extends up to the Gobi Desert, and the Turkestan polecat.

Predators, Reptiles, and Amphibians

The rodents of the steppe are normally preyed on by both predatory birds and small carnivorous mammals. One such mammal is the marbled polecat, which is found from southeastern Europe to the Gobi Desert, across the west and central Asian steppes. Two species of polecats are found on the Eurasian steppes, the European polecat and Turkestan polecat.

Polecats are robust, high-strung animals. They have the agility and strength of the weasel. Though they are smaller in size than pet cats, their long, sharp teeth compensate for their small size. They possess anal glands capable of producing a putrid stench, like that of the American skunk.

When faced with danger, the polecat draws its head back and bares its teeth. The hair on its body becomes erect and it curves its tail over its back to make the contrasting colors of its coat most evident.

With its strong legs and long claws, the polecat digs deep tunnels in the steppe. A nocturnal animal, it comes out at night to feed on small animals. It usually stalks rodents, but it may also hunt birds and reptiles. The polecat lives alone except during the mating season when it joins a female. The pregnant female gives birth after a gestation

The sand lizard is a small reptile common in central Europe and most of Asia. Its Latin name, *Lacerta agilis* means "agile lizard." Despite this name, this little saurian, or lizard, is one of the least agile of its family. Compared to the wall lizard, the *Algyroides* species, or the fringe-toed lizards, it is a slow and relatively clumsy animal. On the whole, the sand lizard resembles a miniature emerald lizard because of its bright green and chamois-brown scales, its rounded head, and its tail, which is proportionally shorter than that of the wall lizard.

period of about nine weeks. Then the female cares for her offspring alone.

The grassy steppe is also inhabited by various species of reptiles and amphibians. One common species is the *Eremis arguta*, a type of roadrunner. Another is the sand lizard, which, like the *Eremis arguta*, is active only in the warm months. When the weather is too warm, these reptiles, seek refuge underground in a tunnel newly dug by rodents.

Of all the snakes, the small Orsini's viper is the most commonly seen. The large Balkan racer can be observed frequently. True to its name, it inhabits the Balkan Peninsula and ranges as far east as Iran. Attaining a length of over 10 feet (3 m) the Orsini's viper is the largest European snake.

Amphibians live in many of the pools and ponds of the steppe. The most commonly found species are the edible frog and the green toad. The unpredictable climate of the steppe poses little problem for the green toad, which needs water only for mating, laying eggs, and the development and metamorphosis (change of physical form or structure) of the tadpoles.

Above: The rose-colored starling, dispersed throughout eastern Europe to the Altai, is perhaps one of the most beautiful and best-known birds of the Asian steppes. It continuously migrates in flocks that number as many as a thousand birds. When threatened by a falcon, they group tightly together to make it difficult for the predator to aim at a single member of the flock.

Opposite: A magnificent bee-eater, pauses with its catch, a grasshopper.

Birds

The birds of the steppe, like the mammals, have developed special adaptations. Their ability to move rapidly on the ground and their tendency to form large flocks are two of their special behaviors.

The rose-colored starling clearly demonstrates these adaptations. This beautiful pink bird with its contrasting black iridiscent (brilliant) head, wings, and tail can be observed from the Persian Gulf to the Altai. This species is almost constantly migrating as it searches for locusts and grasshoppers. A single colony may be made up of thousands of starlings. These starlings nest during May and June, choosing their breeding sites near hordes of locusts and where rocky nesting spots are available. The somewhat fragile nest is composed of grass, small twigs, feathers, and roots.

The colorful blue-cheeked bee-eaters and rollers also thrive on the steppes. The bee-eaters generally move in small groups, hunting locusts and other insects. These are called "coprophagous insects." In contrast, rollers may attack small rodents or lizards.

Bee-eaters nest in colonies, digging tunnels 3 to 6 feet (1 to 2 m) long in the sandy or clay soil. The female deposits five or six eggs at the end of the tunnel in a small section which she filled with grass. The male and female take turns sitting on the eggs and feeding the chicks.

The most notable species of birds living on the ground in the steppe region are the partridges and great bustards. Both the true great bustard and its smaller cousin, the little bustard, were once widely scattered throughout the grassy plains of Europe. Today these birds are in decline because modern farming has reduced the available land on which they can live.

The great bustard is the largest of the European birds. The adult male can weigh up to 35 pounds (16 kg) while the much smaller female does not exceed 13 pounds (6 kg). Groups of these birds spend the day combing the steppes in search of seeds and insects. In the breeding season they also hunt such small vertebrates as rodents, lizards, and frogs. The males are polygamous, mating with several females. During mating season the male tries to attract the female by an extraordinary courtship display. They lift their smaller feathers, such as the wing coverts and tail feathers, to show off the pure white feathers underneath.

Also in this display, the wings are usually lowered until they almost touch the ground. The tail, on the other hand, is

lifted straight up and the head is almost buried toward the back among the shoulder feathers. At the breast, the whitish, bristly feathers stand perpendicular to the body. Finally, the throat sacks are inflated with air.

When they complete this change, the birds look as if their plumage is turned practically inside out and each bird seems to become a soft mass of white feathers.

The nest of the great bustard is nothing more than a shallow depression without any grass lining. It may even be on completely open ground. In mid-April the female lays two to three eggs. It then broods and raises the chicks without assistance from its mate.

Another large bird of the steppe is the demoiselle crane, a species that, unlike the great bustard who chooses several mates, is strictly monogamous.

Outside the mating season it joins flocks of several hundred other cranes. It is distinguished by its beautiful blue-gray feathers and its blackish neck and breast, which

A few of the most typical birds of the Eurasian steppe. *Top, from left to right:* A pallid harrier, hunting; a little bustard in flight; an adult roller (foreground) and its young; an imperial eagle perched on a trunk; a demoiselle crane; a male great bustard displaying its plumage (in the foreground) to attract the female (in the background) during mating season.

are covered with elegant, long feathers. Behind the eyes it has two wide tufts of soft white feathers.

In March, as soon as they arrive on the steppes from their winter homes in southern Asia and Africa, the demoiselle cranes meet in certain locations where they carry out their elaborate courtship ritual. On a section of dry ground, they form a circle. Small groups then take turns in a movement that is similar to dancing. The birds move forward and backward with half-open wings, curtsy, jump, and at times pause in a slight bow. From time to time they stretch their necks, extend their throat feathers, and emit a loud guttural sound. Other species of cranes also exhibit this behavior.

Finally, many raptors, or predatory birds, soar over the steppe in search of small prey. They commonly hunt rodents but will also chase birds like the little bustards. Among the best-known raptors are the imperial eagle, the steppe eagle, the golden eagle, the long-legged buzzard, and the pallid harrier.

THE RED SEA

The Red Sea is perhaps the most extraordinary expanse of water on earth today. Long and narrow, it stretches from the northwest to the southeast for about 1,305 miles (2,100 km) from Suez to the Gulf of Aden. From there it flows to the Indian Ocean. Normally the water is an intense blue-green color, but from time to time it becomes covered with an extraordinary growth of a species of algae called Trichodesmium erythraeum. When it dies this plant gives the water the reddish brown that gave the Red Sea its name.

General Characteristics

No river flows into the waters of the Red Sea, nor does any significant amount of rain fall. For these reasons the waters of the Red Sea are far more salty than the oceans and enclosed lakes. The water is undoubtedly the warmest in the world because it is exposed to so much sun. So much water evaporates that the level of the Red Sea would drop about 6 feet (180 cm) a year if water from the Arabian Sea did not flow into it from the Strait of Bab el Mandeb to compensate for the loss.

The Red Sea formed as a result of two complex phases of the earth's movement. From a geological point of view, the first phase occurred relatively recently—about 50 million years ago. During that phase, the Arabian Peninsula began to detach itself slowly from the African continent. Later during that phase, about 35 million years ago, the Gulf of Suez opened up to form the northern portion of the sea.

The second phase began more recently, only 3 to 4 million years ago, when the two continents moved apart. This separation created new passages in the Gulf of Aqaba and in the southern Rift Valley. The land masses are still separating. The common occurrence of volcanoes and earthquakes during the last 10,000 years are evidence of this movement. Although sea floors are normally very cold, the Red Sea may reach 140°F (60°C) because of the volcanic activity beneath the floor. In some parts, the Red Sea reaches a depth of about 8,250 feet (2,500 m).

During the last glaciation, from 23,000 to 30,000 years ago, the waters of the Red Sea penetrated to depths of 410 feet (125 m) and the salt content increased to the point that most of the coral could not survive. As the polar ice caps melted, the water level began to rise and coral from the Indian Ocean recolonized the Red Sea on reefs formed from fossil remains.

Opposite: Magnificent specimens of shells can be discovered on the shoreline beaches of the Red Sea. Seen here in the foreground are shells of the *Tridacna* genus, or bivalve mollusks.

The map shows the lines along which the Arabian Peninsula separated from Africa, causing the formation of the Red Sea and the Rift Valley. Also shown are the numerous volcanoes and volcanic deposits that are evidence of the relatively recent date of this movement. Lines in the water show how coral structures are distributed along the coast.

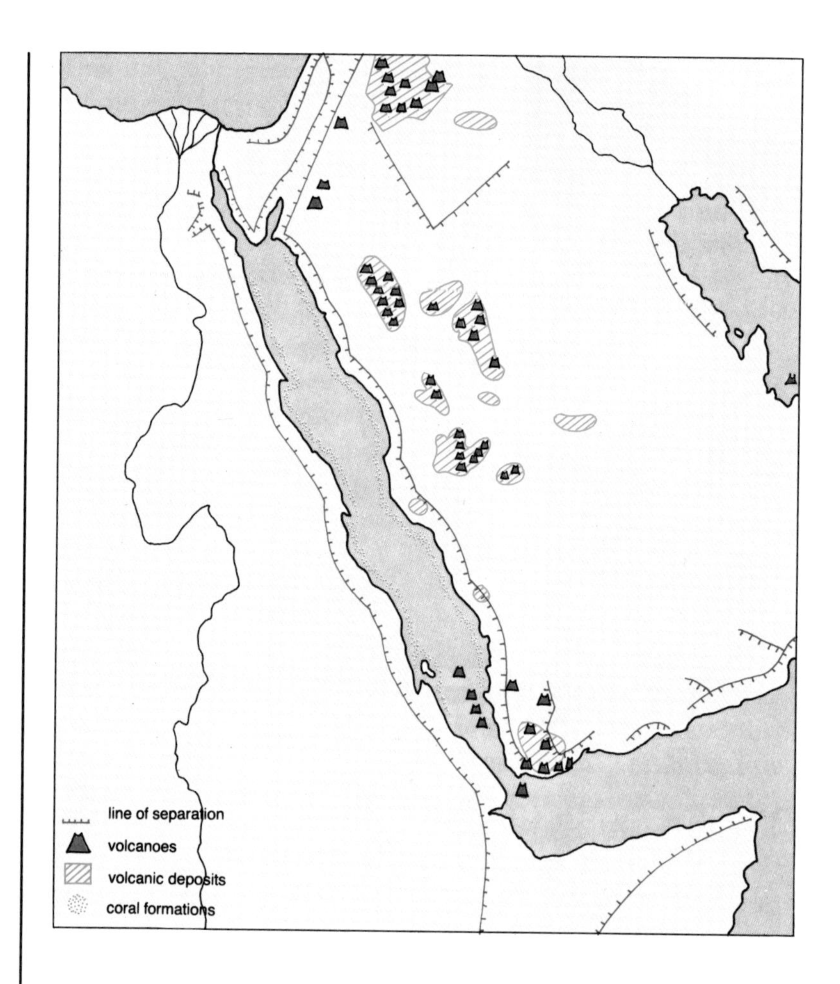

The Suez Canal

The Suez Canal connects two great basins, the Indo-Pacific on one side and the Atlantic on the other. Completed over a century ago, it is one of the world's greatest engineering feats. The Caliph of Baghdad thought of building the canal as long ago as the ninth century B.C., but it became a reality only in 1869 through the work of the French engineer Ferdinand de Lesseps.

The Suez Canal stretches for at least 100 miles (160 km) from Port Said in the north to Suez in the south. For most of the year the current flows from south to north, but in the summer months, from July to September, northwest winds reverse this pattern.

In spite of this, various species of fish have appeared in the south. In the future, the mixing of the two marine populations may change the present ecological balance. Some species have already increased significantly. For example, a

Along the rocky coasts of the Red Sea, stony coral colonies form fascinating flat banks like those visible in the picture. They are made up of the calcium-based skeletons from dead coral. Many coastal areas and most of the islets of this sea are of coral origin and offer scenic views that are extraordinarily beautiful.

species of Red Sea crab, the *Portunus pelagicus*, has appeared in the Mediterranean and is considered a common variety as far west as the southeastern coast of Sicily.

Corals

Today the comparatively small area of the Red Sea holds the largest variety of coral species in the world. There are actually more kinds of coral in the Red Sea than in the Great Barrier Reef of Australia. In the Gulf of Elat, there are approximately one hundred species, among which is the *Stylophora pistilla*. This species alone represents more than 20 percent of the total mass of living coral in the world.

Most of the islands in the Red Sea are coral in origin. The corals and their close relatives, the sea anemones, make up a large part of the type of marine life characterized by being attached at the base. Also known as sessile fauna, these creatures in turn provide particular habitats for a large variety of marine organisms. In order to survive, these little marine coral need warm, clear water that is rich in oxygen.

For this reason, coral reefs are found only in tropical regions, particularly between the Tropics of Cancer and Capricorn. However, they are not found at these latitudes along the western coasts of any continent. This is because cold currents keep the water at too low a temperature there. For example, a cold Atlantic current meets the western

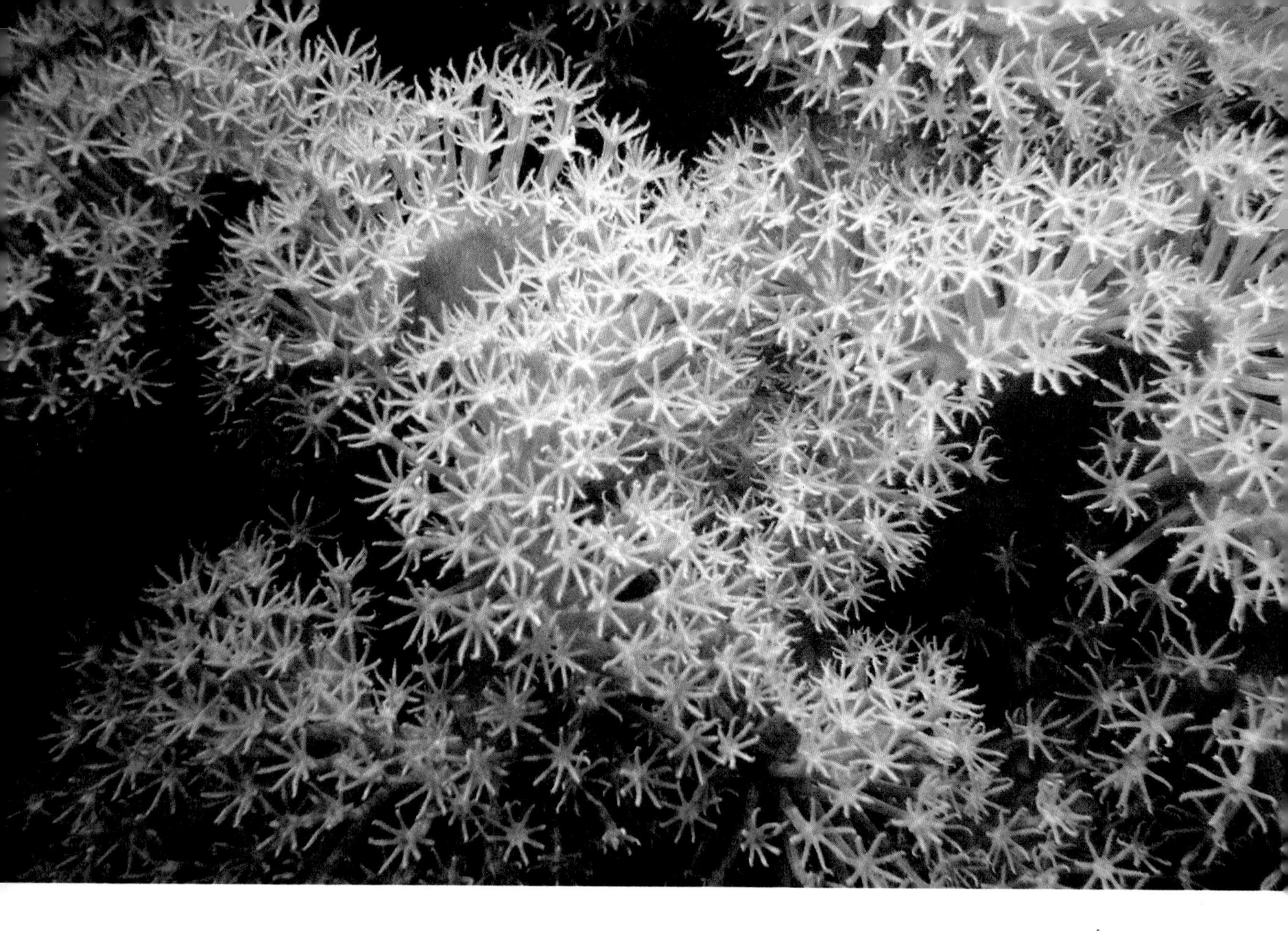

Above: A colony of *Althelia glauca* polyps appears as something from a fantasy.

Opposite, above: This cross-section shows how the stony coral polyp is protected by a calcareous cup-shaped skeleton (wall) that has divided walls, or membranes, called septa. They are like those formed by the soft walls of the polyp itself, the mesenteric septa. Glands along these septa secrete the juices necessary to digest the food that is caught by the tentacles and carried along the pharynx, or mouth, to the internal cavity. Finally, the connective tissue, which grows out of the polyp wall, completely covers it and attaches to other individuals of a colony. This connective tissue allows them to respond together to external stimuli. For example, they may withdraw. In the drawing below, the two middle figures are withdrawing to protect themselves; the one on the left is fully extended, and the one on the right is the remains.

Opposite, below: The multicolored appearance of a seabed in the Red Sea. Polyps may differ in size and colors according to the species of the stony coral. However, their colors are almost always brilliant.

coast of Africa and no coral reefs exist there. On the other hand, coral reefs are abundant to the east in the warm waters of both the Red Sea and the Indian Ocean.

The organisms that make up the coral reef are numerous and varied. Many corals live in a close relationship with zooxanthella, an alga which gives the coral a green tint. This relationship, called "symbiosis," is a method of survival in which two different organisms live in close association with or actually attached to each other. Each benefits from the relationship. In the case of the coral and the alga, the algae obtain the nitrogen they need from the waste products of the coral. In turn, the coral uses in its life processes some of the sugar that the green algae produce through photosynthesis. Below 295 feet (90 m) however, this symbiotic relationship does not occur. There is not enough light to sustain photosynthesis and the algae cannot survive.

Corals are made up of individual organisms called polyps. (At one time, the octopus was also called a polyp.) Actually, a polyp is a coelenterate, an organism characterized by its large central cavity. An octopus is a mollusk. Other mollusks are clams, mussels, and snails. Coral is a

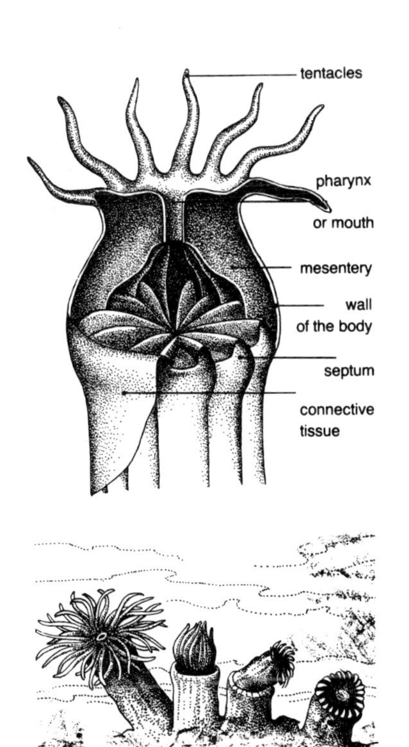

collective name for a colony of polyps. Every polyp has tentacles and a gelatinous (gelatinlike) body, like that of the jellyfish, and it is protected by a skeleton of calcium carbonate that is slowly secreted as it grows.

After the polyp dies, this skeleton remains. As more polyps die, the hard skeleton material accumulates, forming the reef. As new polyps continue to grow on the main colony, the reef grows higher year after year. However, the coral that rises above the surface of the water cannot survive for long. In the same way, coral that is exposed to the sun's rays at low tide will die.

Corals, like sea anemones, are specialized predators that catch tiny prey with tentacles armed with nematocysts, or groups of stinging cells. Under examination, these cells are found to be tiny capsules containing poisonous filaments (thread) with harpoonlike hooks. When the animal is stimulated, it thrusts out the filament, piercing the tissue of the prey. Many swimmers have experienced this type of attack when bumping into a jellyfish, which is a typical coelenterate that has nematocysts.

Coral polyps feed mainly at night when zooplankton concentrate at the ocean surface. Stretching out of their

Stony coral and multicolored fish swim in a coral reef of the Red Sea. Coral reefs can only form under specific environmental conditions. The temperature must be higher than 70°F (21°C) and the water's depth must be less than 247 feet (75 m). Therefore, they are found in the warm seas, especially on the eastern coasts of the continents, which are usually warmer than the western coasts. Besides the numerous species of multicolored fish, many other animals live on the reef, such as mollusks and marine animals of the Foraminifera order. These are single-celled animals that live in shells that they build themselves. Once dead, these animals contribute their calcareous shells to the further growth of the coral mass.

The crown of thorns is a starfish that uses polyps as a primary food source. When too many of these are present, they can cause grave damage to the coral. The remains of the coral are then subject to erosion from the sea and then the lifeless calcareous skeletons are destroyed.

calcareous skeletons, the polyps spread their tentacles in search of their small prey. Once the prey is caught, the food is pushed toward the mouth opening.

Coral polyps reject vegetable material; any that becomes deposited in the gastric cavity (stomach) is not digested. In some corals having particularly short tentacles, the food caught by the tentacles is brought to the mouth by means of vibrating cilia (short, hairlike fringe) designed for that purpose.

The main coral structures of the Red Sea are reefs that follow the outline of the coast and are separated from it

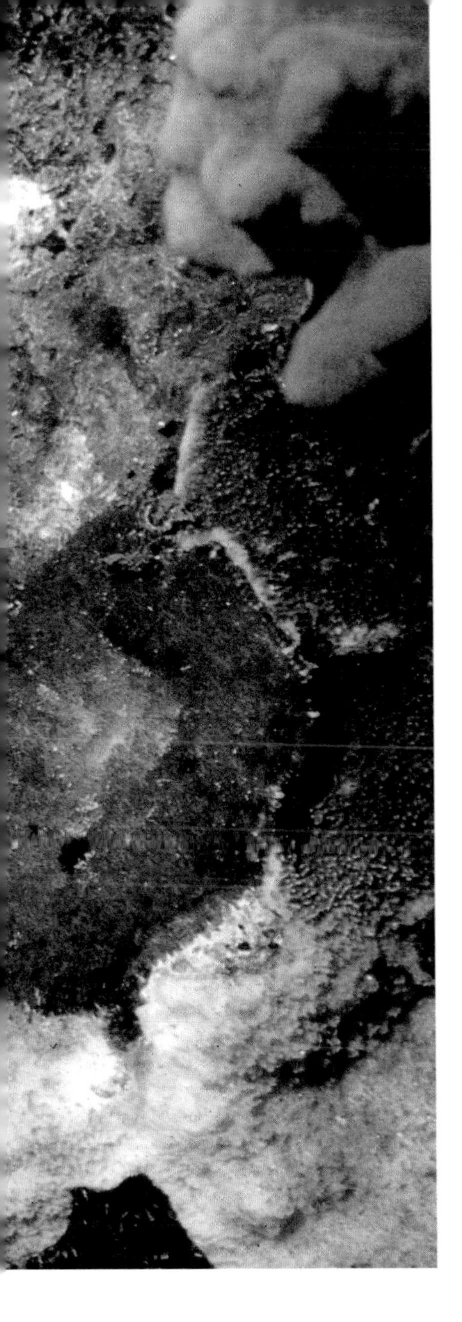

solely by a thin strip of shallow water. Here in these well-protected lagoons, a great variety of organisms prosper. Fish, sea urchins, starfish, and many other organisms find an ideal habitat in these walls built up from the coral skeletons. With their calcium base, the reefs could be thought of as calcareous fortresses. Actually, life is not gone from the reef, even when all the polyps on its surface are dead.

Today, oil threatens the survival of the coral reef communities more than any other environmental factor. Contamination from oil causes the death of a great number of larvae and decreases the polyps' fertility. Animals that eat the coral cause considerable damage to the structure of the reef, too. The most notable of these is the parrotfish, the *Coris*, which is a species of wrasses, and the triggerfish. Other destroyers of the coral are sea urchins, particularly the *Heterocentrotus mammilatus*, and the boring sponges.

The greatest nocturnal predator of coral in the southern part of the Red Sea is the Crown of Thorns, a starfish. It attacks the coral by enveloping it in its large arms, then pushing its own gastric sack towards its mouth and pressing the sack against the surface of the coral. The polyps respond by secreting large amounts of gluey mucus and extending their poisonous filaments. However, within fifteen to thirty minutes, the dying coral tissue swells, leaving behind a cloud of green-brown gelatinous material. After about an hour, the polyps are reduced to semiliquid strands. Only the white, calcareous skeletons remain intact in the water.

Fish of the Coral Reef

The origin of most of the living organisms in the Red Sea can be found in the warm waters of the great Indian Ocean to which it is joined. At the south, the Red Sea is linked by the Bab el Mandebstrait to the Gulf of Aden. Being so enclosed, the Red Sea could be compared to an incubator where many ocean species pause to adapt as they migrate. In fact, most of the Red Sea's endemic species, that is, those that are native only to that area, are related to species of the Indian Ocean. The endemic species make up about 15 percent of the total number of species.

The fish of the coral reef have brilliant colors that fall in beautiful patterns of stripes and patches. The colors and designs may vary widely within a single species. In fact, remarkable changes are often found, depending on the sex or age of an individual fish, on the season of the year, or on the particular location. Or, like the chameleon, these fish

can undergo rapid color changes due to changes in their nervous systems.

In general, many of these fish are very flat. Seen from the side, they are large and colorful, but seen head-on, they almost disappear from view. They can move extremely rapidly in any direction. When danger is near, they may speedily find refuge in one of the many holes formed by the coral skeletons, or they may quickly dart away. They also can stop abruptly to gain an advantage.

Typical of the coral habitats is the brightly colored parrotfish. This fish's teeth are fused together, forming a kind of parrot beak. With this powerful tool, these extraordinary fish break off the calcareous skeletons of coral to feed on the polyps. They also feed on other sessile animals, such as annellids, which are the segmented worms that attach themselves to the coral structure. They may also eat the same algae that grow on the coral. People who visit a coral reef can easily hear the noise of the coral breaking in the teeth of the parrotfish. Parrotfish tear pieces from the coral and grind them in their mouths until all the organic content has been extracted. Then they spit the remains out in the form of fine sand. As a result of this intense activity, both the makeup and appearance of the sea bottom are changed.

During the day the parrotfish move in large schools and grazes on the coral. At night, they separate and hide individually among the coral. It is thought that they return each day to join in a school in order to discourage attacks from predators. When swimming as a school, the fish are so close together that they could almost be mistaken for one large fish.

Few fish in tropical waters look more extraordinary than the zebrafish. Having large, diaphanous (transparent) pink or purple fins, they reach a length of about 24 inches (60 cm). Their appetite is incredible. With their enormous mouths wide open, they stay absolutely still. When unsuspecting little fish approach, the zebrafish sucks them in along with a great deal of water. The fish disappear inside as if they were pulled by an invisible magnet.

The brilliant colors of the zebrafish function as a warning device to predators. This elegant inhabitant of the coral reef is truly dangerous, for its spines have a poison as deadly as the cobra's. These spines extend from the back, or dorsal fin, and are hollow. At the base of these spines are sacks filled with poison. When attacked, the zebrafish shoots out

Called zebrafish, or turkeyfish, for their extraordinary shape and the beauty of their colors, they are actually a deadly danger to humans who touch them. The spines of their dorsal fin, extending from the back, release a deadly poison.

the poison. Just touching the spines slightly is very painful. However, the zebrafish uses the poison only for defense, never to deliberately attack other species of fish.

The scorpionfish and the stonefish are close relatives of the zebrafish and just as poisonous. However, in contrast to the zebrafish, they have a fierce and threatening appearance. They live at the sea bottom and have rough skin that resembles a piece of coral. They also have many poisonous spines on the head and back. They are the most poisonous fish in the world.

The pufferfish has developed a different method of evading predators. This fish belongs to the *Tetraodontidae* family of fish and lives in the coral reefs. As their name suggests, they increase their size by filling their bodies with air or water when danger is near. As they puff up, their thick, spiny skin becomes like a round pincushion that wards off the attack of the hungriest predator. As an added protection, their skin contains poisonous substances.

With spines that resemble a surgeon's scalpel, the surgeonfish is aptly named. A member of the Achanturidae

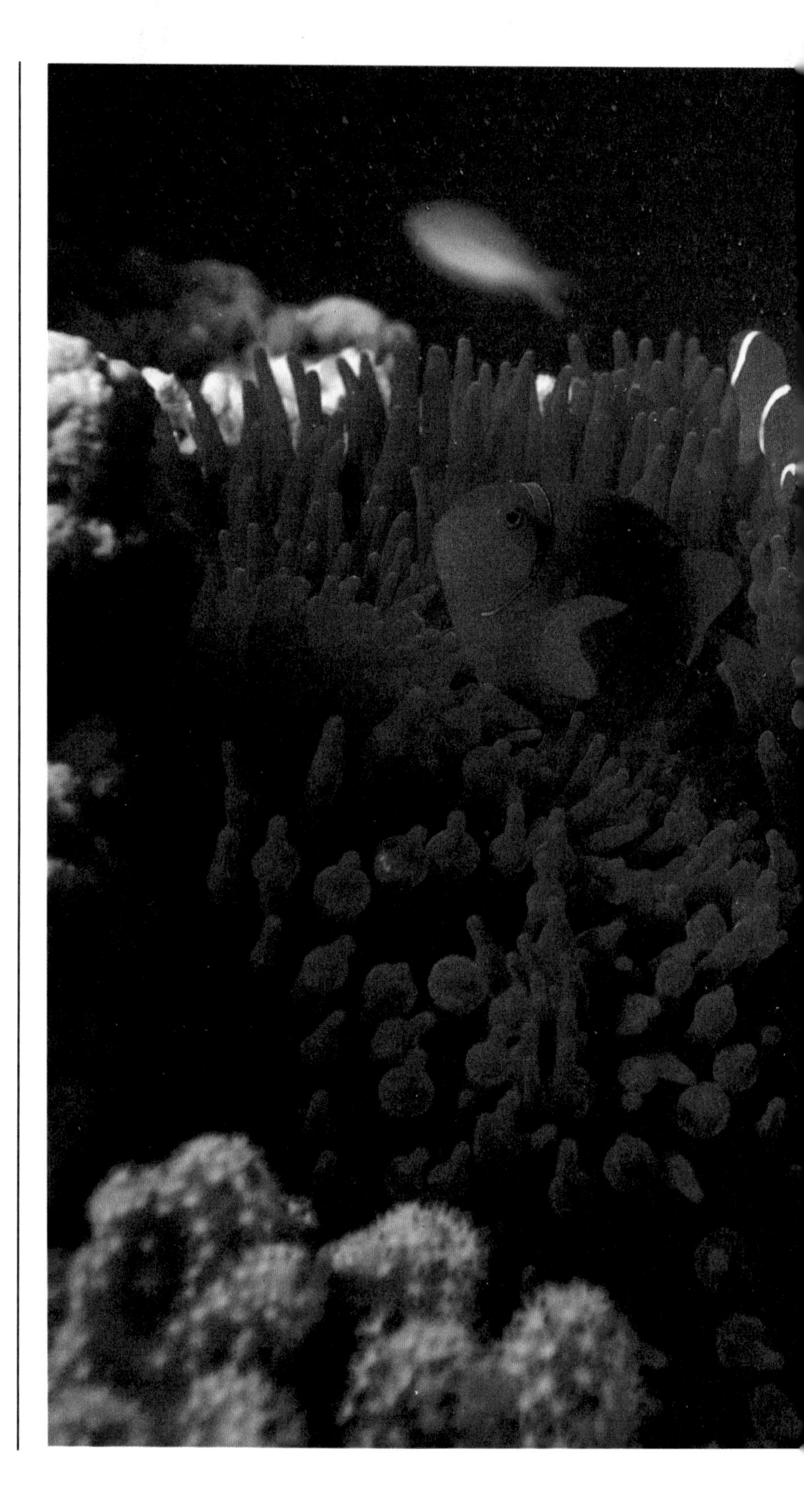

An anemone fish is caught in the tentacles of a sea anemone. The world of the coral reef is studded with strange phenomena. There are amazing examples of creatures that live in association with others, a relationship known as symbiosis. There are unusual and incredible methods of survival, and forms and colors both strange and splendid. A naturalist might compare the coral reef to the tropical forest, an environment that is equally as complicated, rich, and varied.

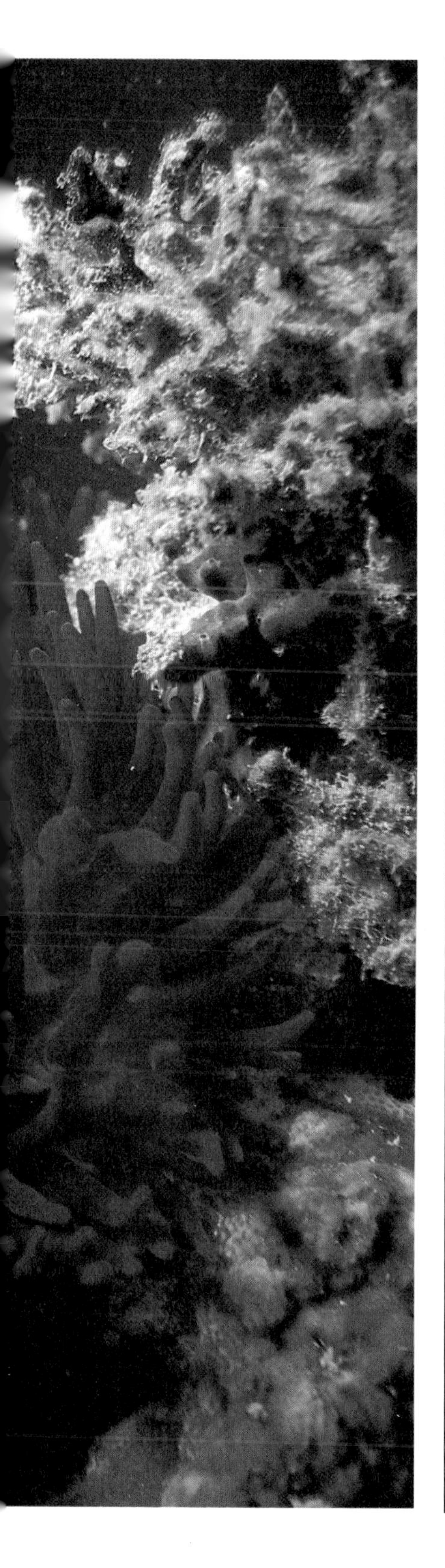

family, it has thick, erect spines all over the body and lives in schools like the parrotfish.

Like the parrotfish, they have strong teeth and eat coral. In the *Aulostomidae* family there is the trumpetfish, named for its long, rigid body and even longer head and snout. Grunts possess a similar shape though they belong to the Pomadasyidae family. They earn their name from the characteristic noise they make when they "grind" their teeth. The noise is amplified by their gas-filled bladder.

Trunkfish are another species found on the coral reef. Trunkfish is the popular name of members of the Ostraciontidae family, which are enclosed in a sort of bony box formed by scales that have grown tightly together. Another strange species is the *Lactophrys bicuspis*, a cowfish which has large spines resembling cow's horns on its head.

Triggerfish are members of the Balistidae family. They have set-back eyes and very strong teeth. Triggerfish are known for having developed a unique behavior that allows them to feed on marine life that have armorlike projections, such as sea urchins. These clever predators strike the sea urchin with a well-aimed jet of water. The sea urchin then turns on its back and the triggerfish moves in to attack the belly, which is protected only by small, short quills. On the other hand, if the triggerfish itself is threatened by predators, it hides among the coral, attaching itself by a dorsal spine in a good defensive position. When the danger has passed, the fish carefully releases itself. It first moves a small dorsal spine, which in turn stimulates the larger one to withdraw.

The brightly colored anemone fish live among the stinging tentacles of sea anemones and so are able to escape predators. In a recent study, it was discovered that the anemone fish are not born immune to the stinging cells of the sea anemones. They become so little by little through a process of adaptation. The anemones themselves benefit from this symbiotic relationship by consuming the food left over from the anemone fish. Also, the anemone fish keep their hosts clean. Except for some brief ventures into the world to search for food, the anemone fish spend most of their lives among the tentacles of the sea anemone. During the breeding season, both the male and female live on the same sea anemone. They also deposit their eggs in a corner that is well sheltered from its tentacles.

Though the fish of the coral reef have developed a vast range of defenses, the predators have developed an equal variety of offenses. Some examples are the scorpionfish that uses "baits," the zebrafish that slowly pushes its prey into blind alleys, and the shark that attacks quickly and directly. Trumpetfish often swim near other large fish, using them as moving hiding places from which they suddenly lunge at their prey.

Groupers sometimes follow European morays and attack the fish that scatter out of the morays' way. Finally, predators have evolved protective coloration that helps them hide from their prey. They wait patiently, blending into the surroundings, or partially burying themselves on the bottom, or hiding in a cave until an unsuspecting fish swims within their reach.

Two cleanerfish are eating food fragments and organic substances they find on the mouth of the triggerfish, which is much larger. Another small fish, very much resembling the authentic cleanerfish, is the false cleanerfish, which attacks the larger fish itself. Nearly the same size and color as the cleanerfish, it approaches large fish with the apparent intention of cleaning them. Once it gets near the larger fish, the false cleanerfish will tear off fragments of the skin and fins. After the large fish have been deceived this way, they are frightened of both the false and the real "cleaners."

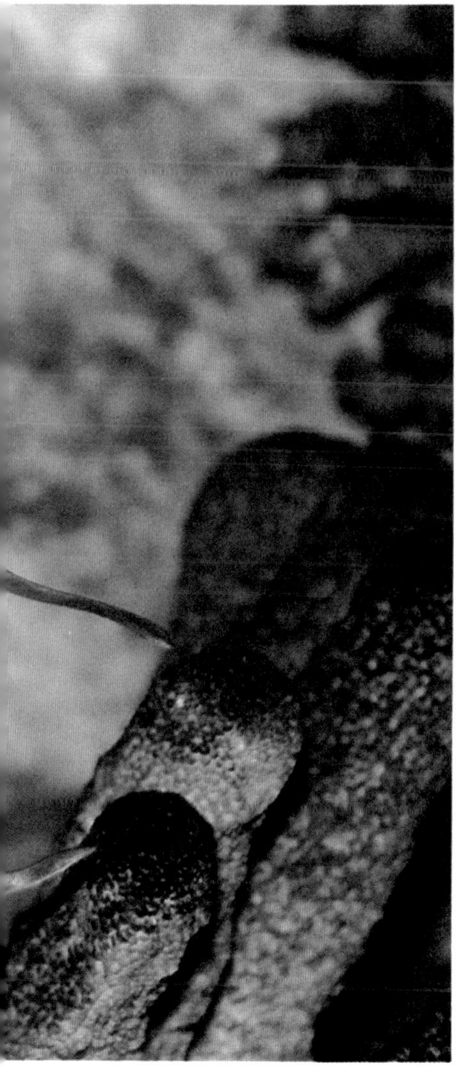

Bisexuality Among Fish of the Coral Reef

Some species of fish of the coral reef have a unique reproductive system based on sexual inversion in which individuals can reverse their sexes. At a certain time in its development, each fish is first a female and then a male, or vice versa. The first condition, known as "protogyny," is much more common than the second, known as "protandry."

Protandry, in which the male changes to a female, does exist among some species, such as the colorful anemone fish. Usually they live in small groups formed by a large adult female and a slightly smaller adult male and various young. If the female is killed or in any way removed from the group, the adult male becomes a female.

Another example of sexual inversion is shown by the cleanerfish, or the species *Labroides dimidiatus*. Many species of labrids organize "washing stations," to which several other fish come to have their fins, mouth, gill slits, and skin cleaned of parasites or food leftovers. At every "station" there is an adult male and about five females. As long as the dominant male is present, the females will not become males. However, if it dies or is removed, the dominant female rapidly turns into a male. Within ten days, it can produce sperm. Sometimes a territory is immediately occupied by another male after the death of a dominant male. The new male becomes dominant, and the female does not become a male.

Mangrove Formations

The plants of the mangrove group thrive in the salty, shallow waters along the coasts of many tropical regions. In the Sinai Peninsula, an abundant species is the *Avicennia marina*, a type of white mangrove. It grows a few feet high between the desolate desert to the east and the blue sea and coral reef on the west. Numerous birds nest on the tops of these plants. Many crabs, mollusks, and small corals attach themselves to its submerged parts.

Many species find the beaches near the mangroves a perfect habitat. Dense populations of ghost crabs, the *Ocypoda sarratan* and the *Dotilla salcata*, are found in that environment. There are also at least three species of fiddler crabs, which are members of the Uca genus. The males of this group typically have one claw that is much larger than the other. During low tide the salty stretches become populated by a great number of crabs. All are busy feeding, digging, and courting females.

MESOPOTAMIA

Mesopotamia, which in Greek means "between two rivers," is actually a vast plain between the Tigris and Euphrates rivers in southwest Asia. To the north, its boundaries are the first foothills of the Armenian Mountains. To the south is the Persian Gulf. Toward the east lie the upland plains of Iran and to the west, Syria. The upland plains of Iran border Mesopotamia on the east, and Syria borders it on the west. The land itself is mountainous. In the north the winters are harsh, while in the south the climate is hot and humid.

Mesopotamia was inhabited as early as 4000 B.C., when the Assyrians occupied the land. Afterward the Babylonians ruled there until their civilization disappeared completely with the fall of Babylonia in 539 B.C.

A Melting Pot of Civilization

The land between the Tigris and Euphrates was originally covered by a dense grove of pistachio trees, while in the Zagros Mountains oaks and junipers flourished. At one time, the entire Mesopotamian region was covered by forest. However, before long it was reduced to an immense expanse of arid land that was useless for farming.

The present dry, untillable land in Mesopotamia is simply the result of eight thousand years of continued human exploitation, or misuse, of the land. All that now remains between the Tigris and the Euphrates is the mineral skeleton of the countryside. Over thousands of years, flooding, irrigation, deforestation (tree cutting), excessive grazing, fire, and war have each had a part in the land's devastation.

The first people to settle in the region were simple hunters and gatherers who lived for the most part in balance with their environment. The people who occupied the land after the primitive hunters contributed to the destruction of their natural surroundings. These people were nomads and farmers who kept herds of domestic goats and sheep. At the end of every summer, they chopped down trees and set fire to the mountain pastures, so that the soil would soak up the autumn rains and grow fresh new grass for their livestock.

Farming first began on the flood plains between the Tigris and Euphrates over six thousand years ago. Farmers using the plow and new methods of irrigation were able to cultivate large areas of land. In those times the region was known as the "fertile crescent," because from the farm products of that land, between 17 and 25 million people were

Opposite: The mouth of the Tigris and Euphrates rivers, where they empty into the Gulf of Persia at Shatt al Arab in a desolate desert setting. Mesopotamia was one of the most environmentally misused regions in the world. In just a few thousand years, it suffered an incredible transformation, changing from a green and fertile land to a sterile desert.

Diagram showing the desertification process. *Top, from left to right:* The original wooded and fertile forest is cleared to open up the land for farming. After excessive farming has drained the nutrients from the soil, grazing animals are brought to that site, and the farms are begun on new, deforested areas. Below, from left to right: As the process continues, the arable, or farmable, areas disappear. The sparse vegetation that remains on the land can feed only the hardiest livestock. Usually, herders bring goats whose grazing eventually completely destroys the land. Finally, the land is completely converted to desert, which continues to advance.

fed. In fact, Mesopotamia was so fruitful that it became famous as a great food-exporting region. Eventually grazing land grew scarce. Herders pushed their sheep and goats closer to the farmers' cropland, causing a permanent dispute between the farmers and the nomadic shepherds over the use of the land. The population continued to grow, however. As the number of people increased, the demand for wood increased as well. People needed this resource both for fuel and building materials. Deforestation, or the destruction of the forest, continued steadily.

The effect of timber cutting on the mountain slopes was greater than the loss of trees alone. With the forest gone, the soil became open to the force of erosion. For example, rain water began to flow down the mountainsides, washing away the rich layer of fertile topsoil. Once this topsoil had eroded, the entire land surface quickly became a barren, stony plain.

The Mediterranean climate also helped hasten the desertification, or drying up, process. The hot, dry summers common to the region definitely did not encourage the ruined vegetation to grow again.

Farming is done in a valley bed, surrounded by desert in the Zagros Mountain region in central Iran. Inhabitants of the region use the underground water that remains in the dry riverbeds and collect it through use of an ancient method of irrigation called the qanat system. Clearly, humans are still determined to farm land that has long ago turned to desert.

The Salt Marshes

For farmers, the excessive salinity, or salt content, of the soil is as serious a problem as the lack of water. As rocks erode in the Zagros Mountains, salt runs off and concentrates in the soil. Winds also bring in small quantities of salt from the Persian Gulf. Normally these surface layers of salt are washed away by rain and carried off to the ocean by the rivers. However, in areas where rain is scarce and there is little drainage, the salt may never be removed from the soil. Then new salt deposits accumulate on the first layers. In very dry climates, this phenomenon is worsened when underground saltwater rises up to the surface through tiny capillaries, or veins, in the soil.

In ancient Mesopotamia, citizens made sure they had enough drinkable water by avoiding excessive irrigation and leaving certain sections of farmland unused for several years in a row. Because of this conservation measure, a deep, dried-out underground layer formed. This layer, which absorbed and held water, also served as a protective barrier against saltwater rising to the surface through capillary action. However, this wise farming practice was soon abandoned and the salt content of the soil gradually in-

White storks and sea gulls fly above swampland in southwest Iran. Today in Iran as well as in Iraq, the humid zones of the Tigris and Euphrates rivers provide a habitat for a rich variety of species, including aquatic birds, wild boars, deer, and marsh tortoises. The animals of this region are still fairly unknown to naturalists, since they inhabit such an inaccessible part of the world.

creased. As a result, fewer and fewer crops would grow in the region. Finally, even barley, which can grow in salty soil better than any other grain, could not survive. Within a few more centuries the fields were transformed into desert.

The only reminders of the once fertile land that had allowed Mesopotamia to flourish were the irrigation canals left buried in the sand. The thriving farming region was ruined and replaced by the desert. This might be the greatest example on earth of how a powerful civilization disappeared because its natural environment was destroyed.

Just as the vegetation decreased or died out completely, the abundant fauna of the region also dwindled. By compar-

ing the fauna of Mesopotamia today with the animals that are pictured in ancient Mesopotamian art, or with the bones dug up during archaeological digs, it is clear that a great many species are now very rare or have become extinct.

Today an animal sanctuary exists in Iraq, in a relatively small area near the Persian Gulf. There, every spring, the Tigris and Euphrates help to form a great marshy expanse of water, mud, reeds, and rushes. In summer the air is invaded by clouds of mosquitoes and horseflies. The water is populated with herons, pelicans, ibises, avocets, eagles, and fisher falcons. In the winter there are also ducks, coots, cormorants, flamingoes, and birds of prey. The birds find the area an ideal habitat, both for its mild climate and for the abundance of food and water.

In spring the marshes start to look like green fields, adorned with white water lilies and marsh buttercups. Countless waterways cross through a large stretch of reeds, some of which grow over 2 feet (6 m) tall. People native to the region use these reeds, not only to weave rugs and mats but also to build huts and houses.

A local legend says that the Garden of Eden was located here, in a lush, green marshland right where the Tigris and Euphrates rivers join. Today the small city of Al Qurnah rises on that location.

Secrets of the Ancient Fauna

By examining records preserved in the temples of the southern cities of ancient Mesopotamia, researchers can draw many conclusions about the animals of the region. The records kept by Sumerians are particularly useful. Among the wealth of facts are lists of words that seem to have been used as dictionaries in ancient times. In each chapter of these dictionaries, animals are defined in specific groups and types. Even more interesting are the pictures of different animal species in the various art forms of the period. (Sumerian civilization lasted from about 3500 B.C. to 2000 B.C.)

In the oldest drawings, animals are drawn clearly and realistically. Human beings are either not shown at all or are drawn in simple outlines. Artists continued to draw in this style until the time of the Assyrian kings, when a new style was observed in the masterpieces adorning the palaces. (The Assyrian empire ended in the early 600s B.C.)

The most-feared animal of the time was the lion. Evidence of this is found by looking at the ancient bas-relief art of the period. (Bas-relief is a type of sculpture in which the figures project slightly from the background.) In these sculptures the lion is shown attacking both humans and livestock. The lion was shown in every period and on every kind of object, from magic charms to wax seals. The most common images showed lions resting or else leaping onto other animals, clawing and devouring prey from the hindquarters. In recognition of the lion's power and savagery, giant lion statues were carved to guard the entrance gates of some temples.

Lions, however, were also hunted by the nobility, and many bas-reliefs show men engaged in battle against these fierce carnivores. As late as the end of the fourteenth century, lions were still fairly common on the swampy plains around the Persian Gulf and in the foothill forests of the Zagros Mountains. The last lion was killed in Persia in 1923. In Syria some specimens managed to survive until 1935, in a remote region near the source of the Euphrates.

Today the few Asiatic lions that remain can be found only in the Gir Sanctuary, a forest situated in the Gujarat region of western India. In 1908 only thirteen specimens survived in this famous protected zone. After decades of strict protection, however, they now number more than 200.

In contrast to the lion, there is a species that has survived even until today, in the vast marshland of the Tigris-Euphrates Valley. This hardy species is the wild boar. According to the religion of the Muslem inhabitants of the

The illustration suggests what the Mesopotamian environment must have been like at the time of the Assyrians, with some of the animals that occupied the region. *From left to right:* The Asiatic elephant, a Mesopotamian deer, a female boar with her offspring, a couple of ostriches and a pair of Asiatic lions.

region, pork was a forbidden food. For this reason, boars were hunted much less than the other large mammals of the region. Large numbers of them still wander among the reeds, searching for underground bulbs, roots, insects, larvae, and worms. They also root in the mud for mollusks, fish, and small ground mammals.

Many birds are pictured on the oldest bas-reliefs and designs of the time. They are generally shown being hunted with bows and arrows, or being captured in great nets. Usually ducks, geese, cranes, and herons are depicted. In those times, ostriches lived on the banks of the Euphrates along with the other birds, and they have been illustrated in great detail on monuments, fabrics, and even on the luxurious robes of the Assyrian kings.

The shells of the ostrich eggs were used as art objects. Some shells found in the royal tombs were adorned with special ornamental patterns and symbols. In addition, the eggshells were thought to hold magical powers.

The ancient artists drew smaller-sized birds without much detail, compared to larger birds. For this reason they are difficult to identify. It is easier to pick out the predatory birds, however, such as eagles and vultures. Eagles were frequently depicted attacking wild goats or deer, which suggests that the ancient people might have trained those birds for that purpose. Some vultures were shown flying away from a kill with the heads of their prey held in their beaks.

CAUCASUS MOUNTAINS

The name *Caucasus* is a Latin form of the Greek *Kaukasos*, a word used by ancient Greek historians and geographers. They might have adapted it from *Kaz-kaz*, a name found on Hittite drawings of tribes that lived along the southern coasts of the Black Sea. (The Hittites were a powerful group in the area from about 2000 B.C. to 1200 B.C.)

An Island in the Desert

In sharp contrast to the flat, desolate plains nearby, the Caucasus region, or Caucasia as it is also called, is a unique area. Its location and geography separate and protect its inhabitants from the extreme weather conditions of the surrounding regions.

Like the Pyrenees, the Caucasus Mountains stretch along a straight east-west line. From the north to the south, they are somewhat narrow. For long distances they maintain relatively even heights. For these reasons the Caucasians are different from the Alps, which have deep chasms (gorges) and passes all along their range. Another notable feature of the Caucasus chain is the location of its highest peaks. They are situated away from the central range on two of the minor chains that extend out to the north and south.

Extending from the northwest to the southeast, between the Black Sea and the Caspian Sea, the mighty Caucasian chain stands as a wall 560 miles (900 km) long, dividing the continents of Asia and Europe. In the past, the range acted as a "barrier" that prevented the people of the Near East from migrating northward.

The Caucasian range also includes two hilly steppe regions that lie to the north and south of the main chain. The first region is known as the Ciscaucasia, and it extends northeast as far as the great delta of the Volga River. The second region is called the Transcaucasia, and it stretches to the Armenian Highlands. Also formed by volcanic eruptions, Transcaucasia rises over 13,500 feet (4,100 m) high. The entire Caucasus occupies more than 170,000 square miles (440,000 sq. km).

The Climate

The Caucasus Mountains are situated on the border between two different climatic zones. Though one is temperate and the other subtropical, the mountains keep these weather systems distinctly separate from each other. The mountains block the movement of cold air masses coming from the north toward the Transcaucasian region. They also

Opposite: A group of hikers climb the divide between the western slopes (the independent Republic of Cabardina) and the southern slopes (Georgia) of the Caucasus Mountains. Rising against the background is the great Betscho glacier, covered with snow. The Caucasus Mountains are known for their gorgeous countryside and unique natural characteristics. Until recently, these sites were not open to tourists.

The alpinelike magnificence of the Caucasus range. These mountains form an effective barrier between the regions to the north, which have a temperate climate, and the southern regions, which have a subtropical climate.

stop southern hot air masses from entering Ciscausasia. As a result, the climate of Ciscaucasia is moderately variable in the west, like that of the steppes, and drier and more variable in the east. Transcaucasia on the other hand, has a humid, subtropical climate, with annual rainfall of 48 to 71 inches (1,200 to 1,800 mm).

The Great Caucasus includes the region on either side of the mountain chain itself. There the low temperatures that occur in the high elevations cause a noticeable increase of rain on the southern slopes. Yearly rainfall reaches a maximum of 162 inches (4,100 mm). At higher elevations, the cold climate is accompanied by high humid-

ity. The tallest peaks are permanently covered with snow.

The climate of the Little Caucasus is similar. The Little Caucasus is separated from the Great Caucasus by a depression in the land that runs along an east-west line in the area known as Georgia. Rain in the Little Caucasus falls mostly in the western sections.

Geology

The basic structure of the Caucasian range is fairly simple. The mountains originated during a great upheaval of the earth's crust, which took place close to 25 million years ago. This upheaval formed what is known as the "alpine geosyncline" (trough in the earth).

Over time, movements of the earth's crust and atmospheric changes have exposed rock that originally lay below the earth's surface. This once-buried crystalline (made of crystals) and metamorphic (change produced by heat and pressure) rock includes schist- or shale-gneiss, and various granites.

Volcanic action also played an important role. The eruptions of the ancient volcanoes Elbrus and Kazbek were especially notable. In the past, lava from their eruptions covered much of the surrounding area. The many hot mineral springs along the western slopes of these mountains are present-day reminders of those eruptions.

The Glaciers

Today as many as 1,400 glaciers exist on the Caucasian mountainsides. Seventy percent of them lie on the western slopes.

The enormous masses of ice and their rivers began as snow piled up over the centuries. Year after year, as the snowy season grew longer and the time of melting and evaporating grew shorter, great deposits of snow gradually built up. Partial melting and hardening caused these giant snow deposits to condense, turning the snow into ice. New layers of fresh snow that fell on the ice also condensed over time. When the ice block reached a certain thickness, it began to slide downward. In this way then, the whole mass inched down the mountainside.

When a huge, heavy glacier moves along a valley floor with an irregular shape, various tensions and forces work on it. For example, the glacier splits and cracks continually, causing giant crevices (narrow openings) and fissures (narrow cracks) to form on its surface. Though it usually moves

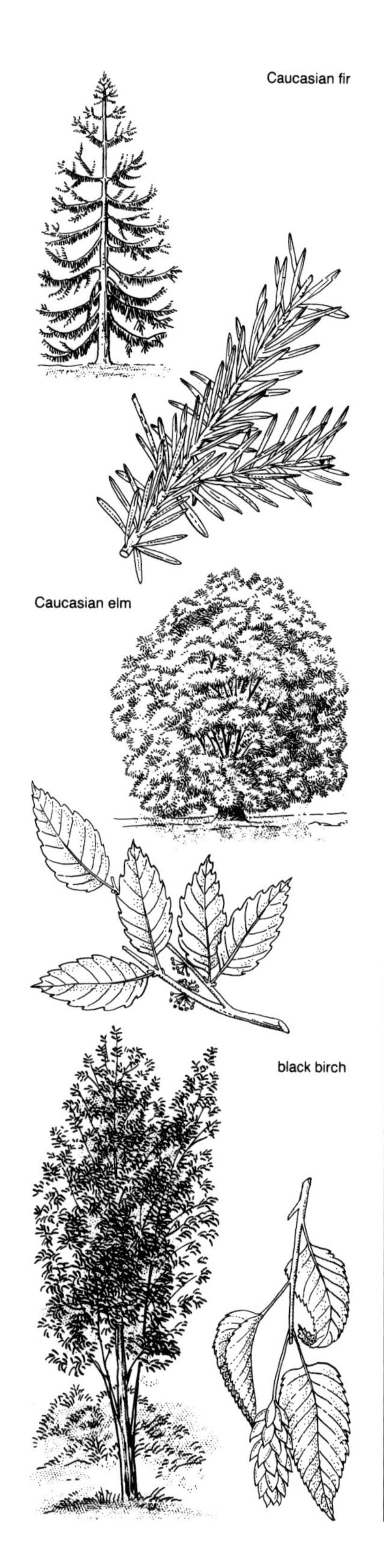

only a few inches (centimeters) a day, a glacier still manages to shift enormous amounts of rock at its front and sides. When this happens vast deposits of detritus, or loose rock materials, form quickly. These deposits are known as frontal and lateral moraines. Over time, the moraines lengthen and extend toward the valley along the path of the glacier.

As a glacier travels, it eventually enters areas where the average temperatures rise higher and higher. Finally, when the temperatures are warm enough to counterbalance the freezing and the melting at the glacier's front, the glacier's forward movement is halted.

The Vegetation

Compared to the barren surrounding plains, the Caucasian countryside displays a kaleidoscope of colors and lush plant life. Different types of vegetation grow in specific locations. For example, the northeast section of the Caucasus has plant life similar to the same area of the Mediterranean region. The mountain forests of the Little Causcasus are much like the broad-leaved forests of central Europe. Further on, the desert steppes of Transcaucasia can be grouped with the desert regions of Asia, while the lowlands of the north are similar to the eastern European steppes.

Within the mild but narrow temperature range of the northwest, a variety of trees grow. Many are species that can also be found in both colder and warmer regions. These trees include ashes, acacias, and oaks. Trees that thrive in colder climates, such as birches and firs, grow alongside them. There are pine trees also. Two species that are usually found in hotter climates are found in these mountains—the Aleppo pine and the classic pine, which are typical of this region.

The forests are thicker on the southern slopes. This side is well protected from the cold winds that blow down from the towering peaks along the mountain crest. These southern forests are nourished by a plentiful water supply that flows from melting glaciers.

The southern slopes of the Great Caucasus are covered mostly by oaks, beech trees, and pines. Dark forests of silver firs, Caucasian firs, and eastern red fir grow to the west.

Farther down, forests of oak, hornbeams, and Caucasian elms grow. Sometimes the branches and trunks of these trees are deformed by the strong winds. Trees that grow on the exposed outreaches and rocky areas are especially subject to the strong winds. In many places they form sparse

The Aleppo pine is one of the two species of the genus *Pinus* that are found in the Caucasus region. Throughout the mountain range, the vegetation exhibits both its alpine characteristics as well as peculiar aspects of the "transition zones." This zone is situated between two very different climates.

thickets just a few feet (meters) high. Though they are sparse, the thickets offer shelter to birds seeking cover at night. Higher in the mountains, clumps of twisted birches can also be found, sometimes near a local variety of maple, or in the drier areas, near junipers.

Junipers have extensive root systems that are essential for their survival. These roots help them resist the wind and absorb all the water they require. Junipers serve an important function in this environment in that they stabilize, or hold down, the soil. They accomplish this largely through the root system. Their great root system reduces landslides and soil slippage.

The Caucasus Mountains are not without predatory animals. In addition to the wolf, shown here on the run, there are also bears and leopards. The Iranian tiger appears to be completely extinct, however, as it has not been sighted since 1958.

The tree line, which is the highest level on the mountain at which trees will grow, varies according to various weather patterns. In the warmer, subtropical zones, the tree line is as high as 7,875 feet (2,400 m). Above this level, limestone rocks cover the ground and only Caucasian rhododendron shrubs grow. Yet these colorful shrubs beautify the landscape and brighten even the highest rocky places.

The Bison

The fauna, or animal life, of the Caucasus is like a green island in an empty sea. The Caucasus offers a great variety of dwellings to its inhabitants. Its location on the frontier between Europe and Asia is ideal for attracting animal species of both continents. In addition, various species are found that are native only to this area.

Misuse of the environment has occurred in these mountains just as it has elsewhere in Asia. In 1925, for example, the magnificent Caucasian bison, native to the region, became extinct because of poachers (illegal hunters) who overhunted this species.

The genus *Bison* includes two distinct species, the American bison and the European bison. Ten thousand years ago, at the end of the last glaciation, the temperature increased in certain areas. This caused the number of European bison to diminish. However, they were found as recently as a few thousand years ago, inhabiting large sections of Europe and Asia where the climate was temperate.

Hunting and the rise in human population have wiped out the rest of the bison. With the spread of firearms, the last groups were completely destroyed. Some specimens are still alive, being raised in captivity in zoos.

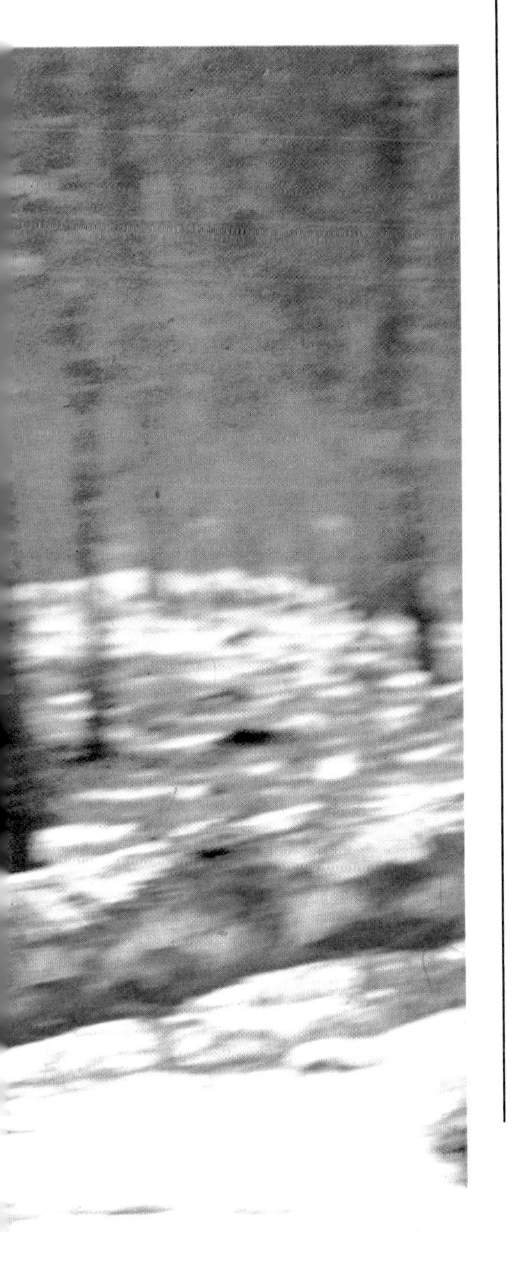

Wild Goats and Chamois

The mountain animals of the Caucasus are well equipped to make excellent use of their difficult environment. They have all the right adaptations that are necessary to survive in the severest conditions. Wild goats and sheep are the best examples. They instinctively know when the seasons will change, and they travel up and down the mountainside at the right time.

Both the wild goat and the chamois, a small, goatlike antelope, live in herds of twenty. These groups consist of young males, females, and their young. Each group is led by an older female. At times other than the mating season in autumn, the adult males form separate herds.

Two chamois on a snow-covered slope of the Caucasus. The subspecies of the Caucasus chamois is clearly related to the alpine chamois. They both originated in Asia, and migrated to Europe during the most recent glaciations.

In mating season, chamois in possession of a harem tend to become violent. Every male marks the surrounding vegetation with a special secretion from glands that are located at the base of his horns. Then he challenges his rivals, one after another.

Gestation, or the period in which the female is pregnant, lasts about six months. In spring, the young are born. Right afterward the herds head up to higher elevations. Here the young can feed on the newly sprouted plants that are particularly rich in nutrients. In the summer chamois generally feed on herbs and flowers. In winter, however, as they descend the mountain, they must struggle to survive on young pine branches, mosses, and lichens.

The wild Asiatic goat is almost certainly the ancestor of the domestic goat. Its domestication seems to have taken place in the hilly, open forests of southwest Asia, between eight and nine thousand years ago.

In addition to the wild Asiatic goat, there are also other beautiful species of wild goats in the Caucasian region. These include the wild goat of *Severtzo* in the western region, and the wild Caucasian goat in the east. Because both animals are well adapted to high altitudes, they hardly ever come down to the forest level. Compared to the chamois or the wild Asiatic goat, these wild goats can stand conditions that are more severe. It is known that they were more numerous during the last glaciation. Then, like the Caucasian bison, they dwindled in number because of the climate, and also because of being continuously hunted. Bolder than the chamois, they tend to come within shooting distance of humans.

Sheep

Goats and sheep are alike in many ways, but in certain aspects they are much different. For example, goats are more agile than sheep. Also, goats have beards and a gland at the base of their tails that gives off a special scent. Their foreheads are more convex than concave, and their horns generally curve backward or upward. Sheep horns usually curve in the form of a spiral.

In general, the goats and sheep that live high up the mountain are larger in size than the same species or related species that live at lower elevations. The animals' larger size is actually an adaptation that helps them survive in their cold, mountain habitats. Because the bodies of those animals grow larger, the increased body mass retains heat. At the same time, the skin, through which heat escapes, increases only a small amount, keeping the animal warmer.

The wild Caucasian sheep is very likely the ancestor of the modern-day domestic sheep. In fact, the bones of this animal have been found along with other remains in excavations of human settlements that existed as long as 7,000 years ago.

Other Mammals

In addition to goats, chamois, and sheep, the Caucasus is also home to deer, roe bucks, and wild boars. Predatory animals, such as the brown bear, the wolf, and the lynx, are found throughout the region along with the abundance of hoofed animals. The leopard is found in this region, but far less often than the other animals.

Birds

The majority of birds in the area migrate to more favorable climates. However, many nonmigratory birds have been identified. One of these birds is the bearded vulture. One of the largest predatory birds in the world, the bearded vulture is still fairly common in the Caucasus. Unlike the true vulture, its head and neck are completely covered with feathers. This vulture is also distinguished by the unique "beard" of pointed plumes on its lower jaw.

This species chooses the most difficult openings in the rocky mountainsides and makes its nest by stuffing branches, twigs, fur, and bone in these crevices. Starting at the end of February, the female lays one or two dark-yellow eggs that sometimes have brown spots.

Like the other big birds of prey, the bearded vulture looks for food by flying along familiar paths at lower elevations. The carcasses of big mammals are this bird's favorite food. When the bird captures a smaller mammal, it swallows the prey whole. However, when it finds the carcass of a bigger mammal, it expertly picks out the marrow from the bone. To do this, the great bird flies up high, holding the bone—such as the thigh bone of a mule—tightly in its beak or in its claws. After rising to 165 to 230 feet (50 to 70 m) the bird drops the bone onto the rocks, where it shatters. Then the bearded vulture selects the most edible parts. This bird uses the same method to split the shell of a turtle in order to eat the meat.

True vultures, such as the griffin and the European black vulture, are also present in the Caucasus. The speci-

Opposite: A griffin vulture perches on its nest. Today, about fifty pairs of griffins, fifty to sixty pairs of European black vultures, and five to ten pairs of bearded vultures make their nests in the Soviet regions of the Caucasus. Larger, more established populations of these great birds can be found in the mountains between Turkey and Iran.

Some typical land fowl of the Caucasus region. *Top, from left to right:* The snowcock, similar to the big partridge and present only on the great Asiatic highlands; snowhens (in flight), closely related to the Caucasian snowcocks; the common pheasant, now familiar in almost all the world. *Bottom, from left to right:* A pair of Caucasian hill pheasants, similar in behavior to their alpine counterparts; the chukar, or Asian partridge, similar to the quail but characteristic of drier regions; and finally, the alpine grouse, very similar to the pheasants found on the flat plains of Asia.

men found in this region make up the most sizable populations of these birds that exist in the world today.

Among the various land fowl found in the area, two unique species exist—the Caucasian snowcock and the Caspian snowcock. Similar to large partridges in appearance, they live in the alpine prairies. Their full, rich voices can be heard every morning and evening, often for several minutes without interruption. Like quail, these birds usually fly on a downward course along the steep mountainsides. Their typical flight is a headfirst plunge straight down. For the most part, snowcocks eat the different parts of grassy plants.

Another type of land fowl that resides in the mountains is the Caucasian hill pheasant. In the winter, this bird stays at lower altitudes, making its home deep in the evergreen forests.

The Caucasian Viper

The Caucasian viper lives in the forests of the western Caucasus. It is easily recognizable by the line of black spots that runs along its back. Like the marsh viper, it has adapted

itself to living in a cold climate. In fact, even at temperatures as low as 37° to 59°F (3° to 15°C), it is able to move around and to hunt its prey, although it sometimes has a little trouble with digestion.

In the winter the viper burrows into the subsoil looking for a moist but well-protected shelter. After finding a spot about 6 to 8 inches (15 to 20 cm) underground, it hibernates. In spring and fall it is active only in the daylight hours. Finally, in summer, the viper moves about at night. Then it searches for rodents' dens, rodents being its main food source.

A territorial animal is one that stays in a specific area. The viper is extremely territorial and, therefore, knows its own small area well. Most important, it knows the exact location of all the different holes and cavities that exist in the vicinity. This knowledge gives the viper an excellent advantage when it must flee from predators.

At the onset of the viper's reproductive season, which is the beginning of spring, the male uses its sense of smell to pick up tracks left on the ground by the female. When he happens upon an immobile female, he begins to shake his whole body rhythmically, sometimes hissing at the same time. Then he puts his chin on her backside, and slides forward on her body, curving himself around the same way she is curved. Continuing to slide forward, he touches her lightly to make sure she is receptive. Then, once he is on top of her, he winds his tail around hers, so as to make a knot. The viper then slides so that the knot moves, finally bringing their two reproductive parts into contact. It takes from one to two hours for the reptiles to mate in this fashion.

Caucasian vipers are strictly monogamous. In fact, a male who has just mated and who wants to gets close to a new partner will be immediately rejected, since the new female can pick up the odor of the "rival." Once a couple is formed, the pair may reunite year after year. This happens even though each partner may live on his or her own outside of the reproductive season. The same couples also remate even though there are many other "strangers," or possible new mates, living in the same area.

THE CASPIAN SEA

The Caspian Sea spreads over 170,000 sq. miles (440,000 sq. km) in the western section of the Soviet Socialist Republic of Turkmen. As such, it is the largest closed body of water in the world. From north to south it spans 745 miles (1,200 km), and it varies in width between 125 and 310 miles (200 and 500 km).

Today the water level of the Caspian Sea is around 100 feet (30 m) below sea level, and it continues to drop even lower. Evaporation is one reason for the drop in the sea level. Water also is lost through filtration into the sand. Though the huge Volga River and other rivers flow into the Caspian, the sea's water is never adequately replaced.

Sea or Lake?

The water of the Caspian Sea is not very salty. Actually, it is about one-third as salty as the ocean. Further, the salt content varies throughout the sea basin. To the north, the water flowing in from the Volga River dilutes the salty water so that the sea water is almost fresh. In contrast, at the southeast, the salinity is high because there are no rivers that flow in and because the hot desert sun increases the rate of evaporation.

On the whole, the Caspian Sea basin has more in common with an immense lake than with an actual sea. Taking that into consideration, what factors have determined the present-day makeup of its marine life?

Geological History

The Caspian, the Black Sea, the Sea of Azov and the Aral Sea all have something in common: they are the only remainders of an enormous ancient ocean, once known as the Tetide. At one time, the Tetide extended from western Europe all the way to China. To the south, it spread as far as India. At that time India was separated from the rest of Asia, and was 60 miles (100 km) south of its present-day latitude.

The formation of the bodies of water as they are known today all began about 500 million years ago. At that time the Mediterranean Sea started to split off from the Tetide. In the next 100 million years or so, rivers carried sedimentary material down from higher ground to the water basins below. Today this material makes up, among other things, the bottom of the Caspian, and also the Kara Kum Desert.

About 60 million years ago the Indian subcontinent collided with the rest of the Asian land mass. As a result, the layers of rock along the crests of the two continents began to

Opposite: Fishermen work along a beach on the Caspian Sea. Outwardly the Caspian appears to be no different from other great bodies of water in the world. However, from an ecological point of view, the Caspian is unusual. One important feature that sets it apart is its water. The composition of the seawater is "halfway" between salt water and fresh water. The saline levels of the Caspian range from very strong concentrations in the extreme southern reaches to only traces at the huge mouth of the Volga River.

Aquatic birds take flight at the mouth of the Volga River near Astrakhan. The huge delta area is the site of many fascinating nature and wildlife reserves. These include the Astrakhan Reserve, which is populated by cormorants, herons, pelicans, swans, and sea swallows. In addition, there is the sea fauna, including sturgeon, herring, salmon, and carp. These species all come to this area to reproduce or wait out the winter.

bend and buckle until they caused the rise of today's Pamir, Tien Shan, and Himalayan mountain ranges. With the formation of these mountains, the sea was trapped on the north side, and a huge basin was created on the interior.

Over the next 25 million years, the eastern rim of the basin gradually began to lean toward the upper edge of the Indian subcontinent. As the land continued to press on the eastern side of the basin, water from the basin slowly started to drain out. The basin itself split more and more, until it eventually divided into the Caspian and the Aral Seas as they are today.

Up until 12 million years ago, the Caspian Sea was connected to the Black Sea by a famous land depression known as the Manyck Trench. This trench was finally destroyed by the rise of the Caucasian Mountains, which completely divided the two basins.

During the Quaternary period (2 million years ago to the present) a great many glaciers inched across the Russian plains and the bottom of the Caspian Sea. These glacial

phases left their marks in the form of terraces on the surface.

Today these terraces show us the coastal lines of the past. The results of the glaciers are especially evident when one looks at the topography (surface features) of Turkmenistan, which is lined with long, shallow basins.

The Gulf of Kara-Bogaz

A smaller basin extends out from the east Caspian basin. The two bodies of water are connected by a narrow, bottleneck-shaped channel. This basin represents one of the most spectacular natural phenomena of the world. It is known as the Gulf of Kara-Bogaz.

This "lake" is about 37 miles (60 km) wide, and at its deepest point drops to 14.8 feet (4.5 m). It contains twenty times more salt than the Caspian. Water from the Caspian pours into it continually through a churning torrent that to this day is the only known example of saltwater rapids on earth.

When the waters flow in from the Caspian, the Kara-Bogaz becomes an enormous cauldron (boiling kettle). The desert sun heats up the surface water, which actually evaporates faster than it rushes in from the larger basin. The whole bay area looks like a prehistoric landscape.

The blinding-white sodium sulfate that constantly washes up on the shore makes the beach look as though it is covered with snow. In winter, low temperatures cause the dissolved salt to crystallize and form a white band on the surface of the water.

Ancient Inhabitants and Recent Immigrants

Today, animal life in the Caspian Sea is represented by marine forms and lake or river forms. In other words, there are examples of saltwater fish and organisms and freshwater varieties. However, because of the difficult, "intermediate" conditions in which they have to live, the animals that are absent stand out more than those that are present. For example, among the groups that have managed to survive in water that is not quite sea water or lake water are certain herring *(Clupea)*, various sponges *(Amorphina)*, mollusks *(Cardium)*, protozoa *(Rotalia)* and *(Textularia)*, and others.

Many native species exist in spite of the difficult environment. These include protozoa, sponges, and mollusks and fish of the genuses *Gobius*, *Benthophilus*, and *Cobitis*. One species of mammal is native to the area—the Caspian seal.

Flowering lotus bloom in the Astrakhan Reserve. At one time this aquatic plant was widespread on the Nile River. Today it can be found in Asia, America, and Europe. It grows at a rapid rate in the swampy areas of tropical and subtropical regions, sometimes creating a serious ecological and economic problem. The vast fields spreading over the water make an ideal habitat for certain aquatic birds, especially a species known as rails.

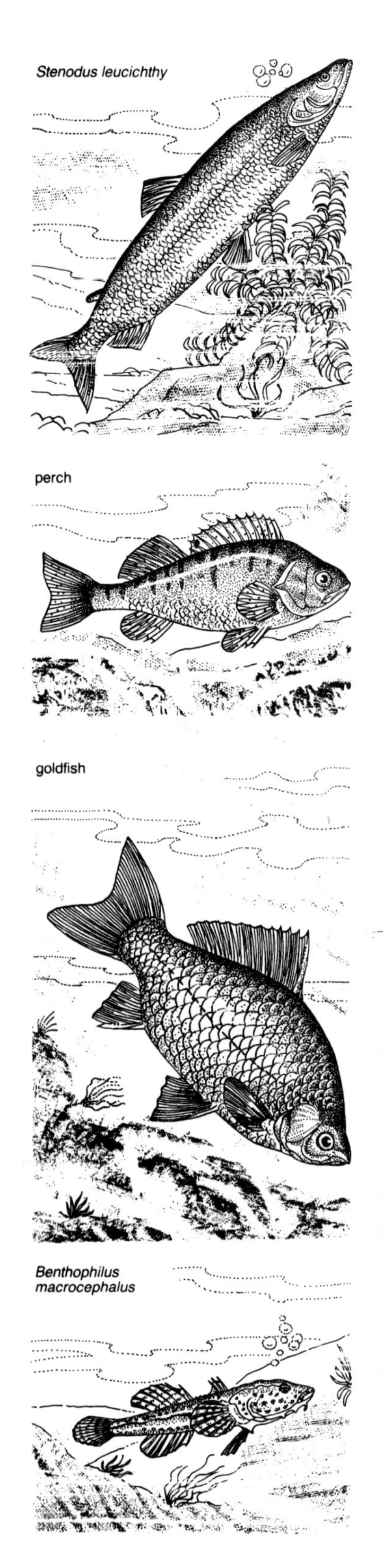

Fish

To survive in the salt environment of the Caspian Sea, some fish have adopted a very simple system. When conditions become too unfavorable, they move to a more suitable area. The fish have a wide range of aquatic environments from which to choose—from the fresh water flowing in from the Volga River to the very salty waters to the east and southeast.

Some species stay in the Caspian for the major part of the year and migrate to the rivers in the reproductive season. Typical examples in this group are sturgeon (with the exception of sterlet), salmon of the Stenodus *leucichthys* species, and certain herring. A second group of semimigratory fish is made up mostly of those that live in less salty zones. They travel to the fresh water areas only to reproduce. These include perch, carp, and pike. Certain members of this group live only in the fresh water at the mouths of the rivers. To reproduce, they swim up the river, looking for water that is more oxygenated. These fish include bream, dace, and fish of the *aspius* species.

A third group is made up simply of river fish that occasionally end up in less-salty areas of the Caspian. They are tench, goldfish, and sterlet. Finally, a fourth group includes marine fish that live in the salt water and rarely venture into fresh water. This group is made up of herring, pike, perch, certain gudgeons, and *Benthophilus*. Some of these fish head toward the coasts to reproduce. Others swim from the south and south-central Caspian waters to the less salty northern zones. Marine pikeperch and various herrings in this group never enter fresh water. They represent typical examples of some of the surviving species from the ancient Tetide Ocean.

Herring Migration

Of all the species of fish found in the Caspian, the herring and its annual migration patterns have been studied the most. The different species in the herring family are famous for their wide variety of forms.

In the winter months the herring benefit from the warm water currents that begin off the Iranian coast and meet in the southern and central parts of the Caspian. With the arrival of spring, however, certain species swim toward the coast, while others migrate to the fresh northern waters. At the beginning of April, when their glands start to develop, the *Caspialosa volgensis* and *Caspialosa kessleri* species

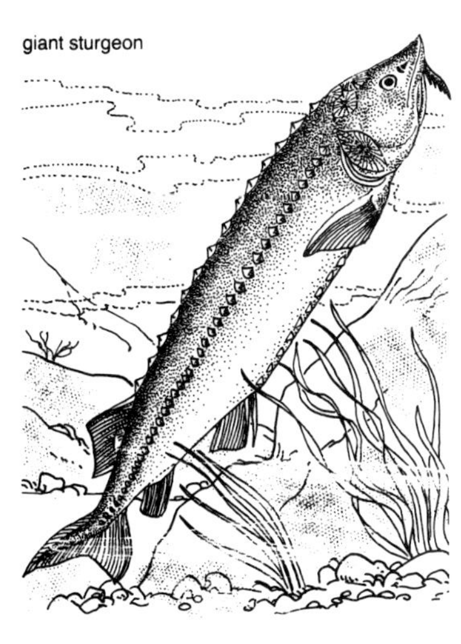

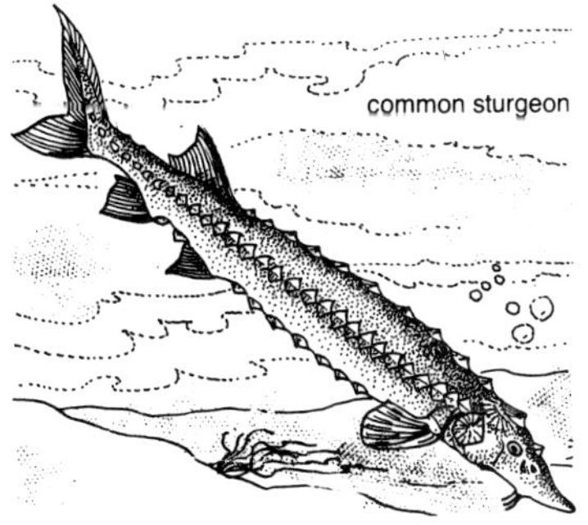

enter the Volga River and swim upstream. The first of the species swims all the way to Gorky, while the second reaches only the lower Volga, as far as *Sarato.*

In this one large habitat, various behaviors can be studied within a group of different but closely related species. A series of gradual transitions can be observed. One can start with the true migratory specimens and end with fish that are marine in the strictest sense. Between the two extremes, examples of fish that exhibit various degrees of each behavior can be found.

In summer, however, the great majority of herring reunite in the northern waters of the Caspian. They are joined by other migratory fish, which have just come down the Volga and other rivers flowing down from the Ural Mountains. Here, in these northern waters, they drop their eggs. As soon as it gets cold, the young are the first to leave, and the adults follow soon after.

The "Pearls" of the Caspian

The most typical examples of ancient sea fauna in the region are the members of the Acipenseridi family. Sturgeon belong to this group. Unlike their ocean ancestors, they spend almost all their lives in relatively fresh water. This fish is easily distinguished from any other by its pointed snout. In front of the mouth, on the underside of the head, are four protrusions called "barbels." The sturgeon's unique snout is a useful tool for capturing larvae and mollusks lying on the sea bottom.

The giant sturgeon is the largest representative of this group, weighing up to 2,425 pounds (1,100 kg). As many as 440 pounds (200 kg) of eggs can be found in a sturgeon at one time. The caviar produced from these eggs is famous in every part of the world.

While it is true that humans catch sturgeon for their caviar, it is also a fact that such animals as herring and other Caspian Sea fish have learned to pursue this great resource. Above all, there are the birds of the region. The most notable of these is the common cormorant, well known to local fishermen. Other species include the Pygmy cormorant, the common pelican, the Dalmatian pelican, red and gray herons, and various species of horned grebes and gulls.

Another fish-eater is a mammal that can be considered one of the most unlikely immigrants to these waters: the Caspian seal. This seal resembles the arctic seal from which it originated. The Caspian seal feeds mostly on gudgeons,

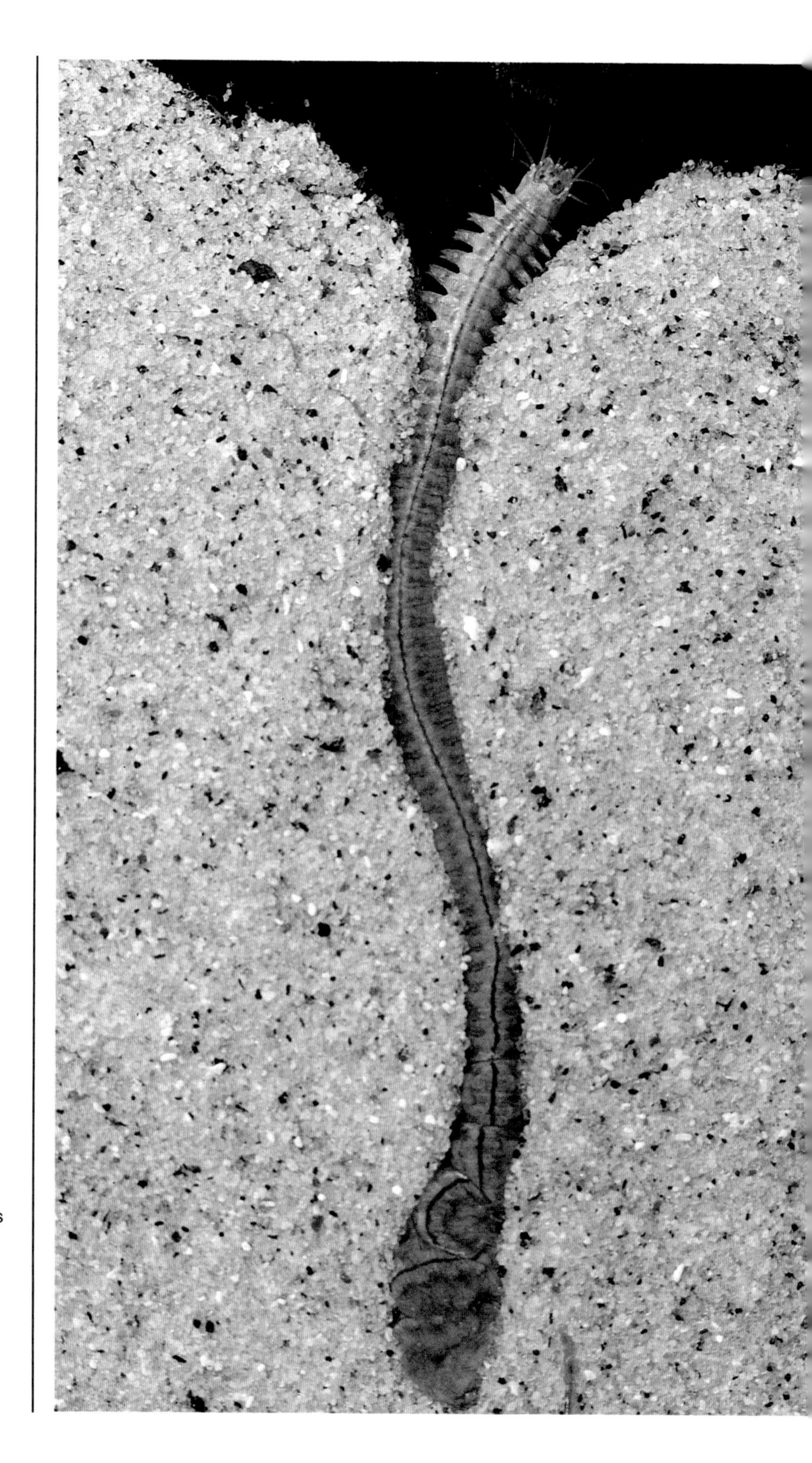

A segmented marine worm classified as *Nereis diversicolor* is photographed through a glass plate in its hole in a sand bed. Known by sea fishermen simply as "fishing worms," these small animals form the base of many food chains among marine animals. When these worms are present, fish populations increase substantially in number, since the worms provide a perfect and abundant food source.

The common cormorant is among the aquatic birds that breed in large numbers on the shores of the Caspian Sea. It thrives on the sturgeon, which is a rich food source found in abundance in the Caspian. The cormorant species is widespread and is generally found living in groups along the world's coastal zones, great lakes and lagoons.

herring, crustaceans, and sprat. In autumn the seals migrate north to await winter and form colonies on the ice. During this time the seals prepare for the reproductive season, which occurs in February and March. The offspring are born the following January.

A Successful Introduction

The constant increase in the exploitation of sea resources has sometimes caused imbalances and severe reductions of certain animal species. To deal with this situation, new species have frequently been introduced. Although these outside species are not native to the region, they are useful from an environmental and economic point of view.

One of the most successful attempts of this type was the introduction of segmented worms of the *Nereis* genus into the Caspian Sea between 1939 and 1941. These worms were intended as a food source for the important commercial fish breeding in the waters.

The Caspian Sea has particular conditions, and its only inhabitants are those animals that can survive such conditions. As a result there are many ecological "niches" that have remained open. Consequently the *Nereis* worms had no trouble finding a place in which to live. They quickly inhabited the vast undersea expanses, which were practically deserts of mud. Within these muddy stretches there existed abundant organic deposits on which they could feed. The result was that their population exploded. By 1948, the worms already occupied a 12,000-square-mile (30,000-sq.-km) area and were the third most numerous invertebrate species in the Caspian.

During their first year of life, these animals stay hidden in the mud. They emerge into view in their second year but only for the purpose of mating. Almost as soon as they abandon their dark, peaceful hiding places, however, they are eaten in great numbers by fish and birds. The result of their introduction has been a dramatic increase in the animal life on which the human economy greatly depends.

GUIDE TO AREAS OF NATURAL INTEREST

Travelers to southwest Asia today find it one of the least accessible places in the world. This area is difficult to explore, even for the region's native inhabitants. Armed conflicts often break out in certain regions, making passage through those areas inadvisable or impossible. Also, obtaining a visa is frequently difficult, even for those areas where conflict is less heated. For those who wish to journey outside the cities to explore the plant life, animal life, and countryside, it is even harder.

Visitors to this part of Asia will find some of the earth's hottest and driest regions. For the lucky few who do manage to visit there, it is worth mentioning some basic travel rules. It is wise to bring light clothing, sufficient water, a first-aid kit, and a vehicle complete with extra parts and an expert mechanic. Cameras must be kept well protected from sand, and film should be kept in a heat-resistant case, or protected from direct sunlight.

Spring and autumn are the best seasons for travel in this part of the world. In summer the heat can get truly unbearable. In winter nights are often very cold, and the days become very short. For travelers who love nature trips and want as much daylight as possible to spend outdoors discovering the scenery, the winter days may be too short.

The largest number of nature parks in Western Asia are found in the Soviet Union and in Iran. In the Soviet Union an efficient park travel organization exists that serves at least some of the country's 145 national parks and nature reserves, known as Soviet Zapovedniki.

Some of the Soviet Zapovedniki are managed much like the national monuments in the United States. Others are more like wildlife refuges. Only seven bear real resemblance to national parks. In all seven parks there are vast wilderness areas. Hunting, fishing, and wood cutting are completely prohibited in all of these reserves.

Many of these parks and reserves were specifically developed to protect certain animal or plant species. Generally speaking, the basic objectives of the system are the same: to conserve the natural characteristics of the territory and to develop research in the field of natural science. The Soviet Zapovedniki, therefore, are usually equipped with science labs, museums, and specialized staffs.

There is no doubt that nature conservation is one of the top priorities in the Soviet Union. This is true even if tourism in the area is ranked much lower than tourism in similar parks and preserves in the Western world.

Opposite: The "earthen pyramids" of the Cappadocia in Turkey are the final remains of an erosive cycle in the desert areas. They escaped total disintegration due to the giant stone boulders that remained balanced on their peaks and thus protected them. If these unique coverings had fallen, the pyramids would have crumbled completely from the combined erosive forces of water, wind, and sand.

The map shows the huge geographic region dealt with in the book, along with the many territorial divisions.The largest number of parks and reserves is in the Soviet Union and Iran where a comprehensive conservation policy was begun before 1981. Many national parks and reserves are also found in Israel, but they are not indicated on this map because they belong to the Mediterranean region. Setting aside land for the purpose of conservation is, for the most part, still a thing of the future for many of the other countries. The exploration of some of these natural areas is still ahead and could hold some pleasant surprises.

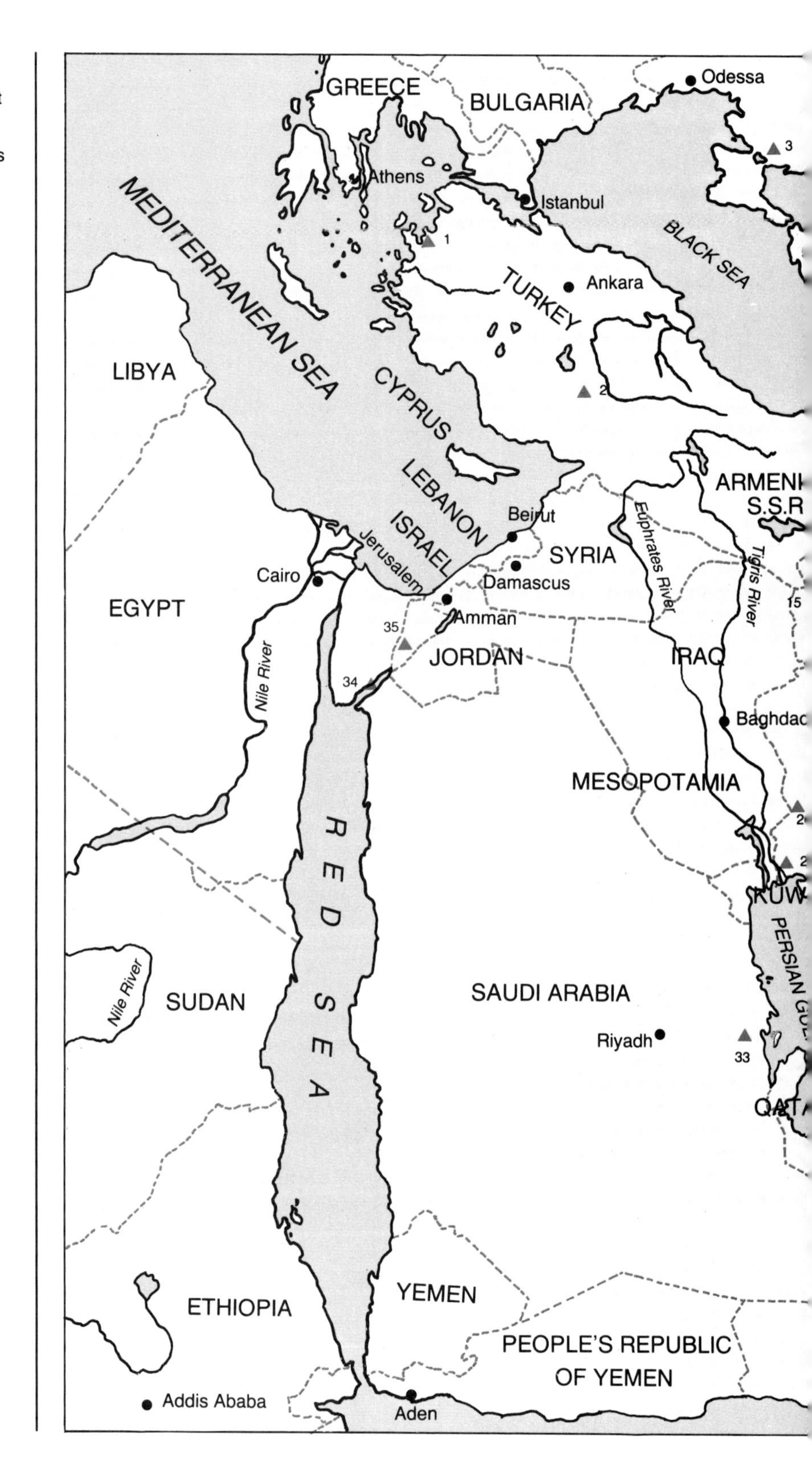

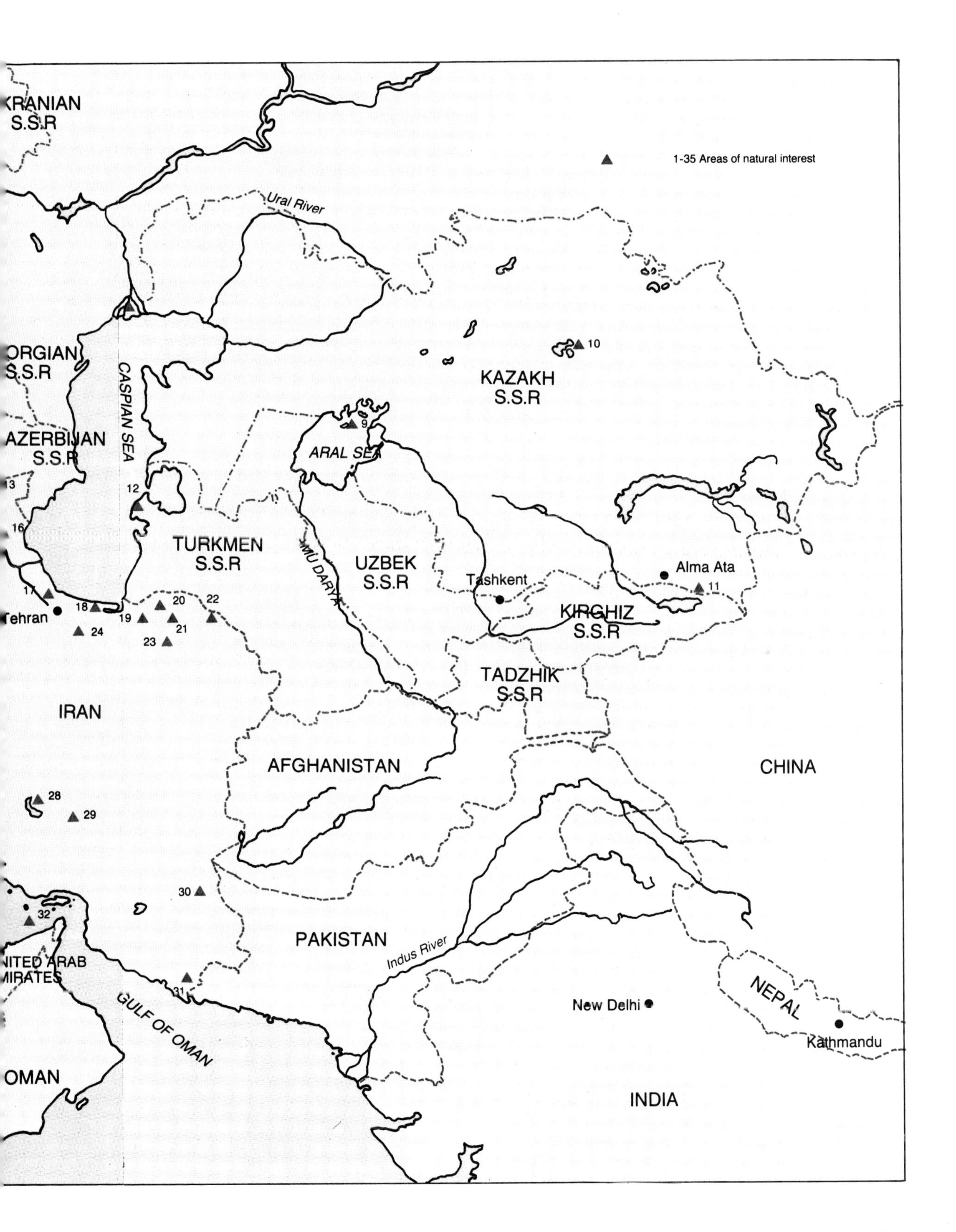
KRANIAN
S.S.R
1-35 Areas of natural interest
Ural River
ORGIAN
S.S.R
CASPIAN SEA
AZERBIJAN
S.S.R
KAZAKH
S.S.R
ARAL SEA
AMU DARYA
TURKMEN
S.S.R
UZBEK
S.S.R
Tashkent
Alma Ata
KIRGHIZ
S.S.R
TADZHIK
S.S.R
Tehran
IRAN
AFGHANISTAN
CHINA
PAKISTAN
Indus River
NITED ARAB
MIRATES
GULF OF OMAN
NEPAL
New Delhi
Kathmandu
OMAN
INDIA

TURKEY

Dumanli (1)

Before reaching the Panfilia plain and the sea, the waters of the Anatolia Plateau have to cross the Tauro hills. The flow is mostly underground. As they pass under the hills, they merge and form the Manavgat River, which ultimately surfaces at an altitude of 4,430 feet (1,350 m). The water that rushes out is known as the Carsican Spring of Dumanli, the greatest and most spectacular natural fountain in the world.

Urgup (2)

The Urgup Valley is typical of the Cappadocia that was carved out by erosion. The area exhibits different kinds of rock formed from the effects of erosion. Springs and streams carry down tufa rock, which was later covered by layers of strong, resistant rock. Because of this protection, the tufa rock mounds never crumbled, and today they form the bases of the great "earthen pyramids" and "mushrooms" that still exhibit their protective coverings.

SOVIET UNION

Askaniya Nova (3)

Spread out over 40 sq. miles (100 sq. km) in the southern Ukraine, this park preserves a fragment of the original grassy steppe that once covered vast areas of eastern Europe and Asia. A great part of the land is dedicated to wildlife preservation, however. Animals threatened by extinction are kept in large enclosures on the territory. Protected animals include the Przewalski's horse, the onager, the ostrich, and the Indian antelope.

Native animals include the suslik, jerboa, hamster, and bobak marmot. Counted among the park's birds are skylarks, meadowlarks, rose-colored starlings, gray partridges, royal and pond eagles, bustards, and moor hens. The most characteristic flowers are tulips (red), irises (violet) and peonies (dark red).

Ukraine Steppe (4)

Three small regions near the Azov Sea make up this preserve, which spreads over an area that does not even total 6.5 sq. miles (17 sq. km). Its vegetation and wildlife are typical of the steppes, including the bobak marmot, gray partridge, skylark, pallid harrier, rose starling, and Orsini viper.

Kavkaz (5)

Stretching over 1,026 sq. miles (2,660 sq. km) in the most western part of the Caucasus (Kavkaz) near the Black Sea, this preserve combines the goals of scientific research with those of tourism.

Since it is situated practically on the edge between the humid, subtropical climate zone of the Black Sea and the drier, cooler climate of the north, Kavkaz has a rich and varied fauna.

Animal life in the area numbers 58 mammal species and 192 species of birds. Of these bird species, 121 nest in the region. The mammal species include the European bison, the tar or mountain goat, the roe buck, the wolf, the lynx, the otter, the badger and, occasionally, the leopard.

Teberda (6)

Situated to the west of Mount Elbrus, and 350 sq. miles (903 sq. km) in size, this preserve is the second largest of the thirty-five preserves in the Caucasus region. It is also of special interest to visitors, since the Tourist Bureau provides official, detailed walking tours. Among the animals one can see are the chamois, tar, bearded vulture, Caucasian snowcock, Guldenstadt red-tailed thrush and Kruper woodpecker.

Satapliyski (7)

This preserve is situated at the site of a beautiful Carsican cavern. It is about 1,970 feet (600 m) long and located northwest of Kutaisi, near the small city of Tskhaltubo (Caucasus). The surrounding territory is dominated by a forest of beeches and yew trees. Interesting animal life can be found both inside and outside the cave.

Astrakhan (8)

This 170-sq.-mile (440-sq.-km) preserve is within the delta of the Volga River on the Caspian Sea. It boasts countless little lakes, lagoons, canals, and other waterways.

In the delta waters various migratory fish arrive in mating or winter seasons. Among these species are sturgeon, herring, salmon, and carp. Among the mammals found are the wild boar and the otter. Birds include cormorants and herons, ruddy duck, the large sea swallow, black-footed sea swallows, the white spoonbill, the leech-eating sea swallow, and the wild goose.

Barsakel'mes (9)

The Barsakel'mes preserve was established on an islet 71 sq. miles (184 sq. km) in size, in the western part of the Aral Sea. It has a near-desert climate, with only 4 to 8 inches (100 to 200 mm) of rain a year. The vegetation includes short-lived desert plants as well as hardier types. Animal life includes the ground squirrel, red and corsac foxes, stone curlew, black-winged stilt, sheld duck, and orange-headed bunting.

Kurgal'dzino (10)

Extended over 715 sq. miles (1,852 sq. km) in the Soviet Socialist Republic of Kazak, this preserve is made up of vast steppe areas between the Nura and Kulan-Utpes rivers, and the Kurgal'dzino and Tengiz lakes. The vegetation is typical of these grassy, scrubby steppe regions, with brushwood, wheat grass, Bromus, straw, and artemisia. Wildlife is found mostly near the lakes. They provide dwellings for flamingoes, swans, geese and gulls.

Alma Ata (11)

This preserve is in the central part of the mountain peaks called Zailisky Alatan (hills of Tien Shan). It spreads out over 345 sq. miles (895 sq. km) at elevations that vary from 1,312 to 15,063 feet (400 to 4,591 m). Fauna includes two species of crow, a marmot, the ermine, the beechmarten, the wolf, the lynx, the deer, the wild goat, the roe buck, the bearded vulture, the royal eagle, the Himalayan snowcock, the Indian partridge, and many other birds.

Krasnovodskiy (12)

Spanning nearly 1,000 sq. miles (2,600 sq. km) on the southeast coast of the Caspian Sea, this preserve was established in a vast coastal zone that includes dunes, lagoons and islets. The vegetation is made up mainly of short-lived plants native to arid regions. The fauna contains many species, including the wolf, the jackal, the honey badger, the goitered gazelle, the sea eagle and the ruddy duck.

IRAN

Arasbaran (13)

Located in a mountainous zone of the Caucasus bordering the Soviet Union, this preserve was begun as a wildlife refuge on a land surface of 1,467 sq. miles (3,800 sq. km) The flora is varied, since it is affected by the Mediterranean climate conditions to the west, the Caspian Sea on the north, the steppes to the south, and the mountains at its highest elevation. The animal life includes wolves, bears, lynxes, wild boars, deer, sheep, and wild goats, Caucasian hill pheasants, Caspian snowcocks, alpine grouse, and gray partridges. The pheasant, which is a true native of this region, is also found.

Kiamaki (14)

This preserve represents another typical dry, mountainous steppe region in the Caucasus. It borders the Soviet Union, on a land surface of 325 sq. miles (840 sq. km). Animals within its wildlife refuge include wolves, jackals, bears, wild cats, caracal, leopards, storks, turkey vultures, and bee-eaters.

Rezaiyeh (15)

Only 16 feet (5 m) deep and very salty, this lake is the most extensive in all of Iran. It contains over fifty-six islets, all covered with salt or overrun with steppe vegetation. A national park has been established. It contains steppe and Mediterranean-type forests. Its fauna is composed of wild sheep, partridges, Indian partridges, sheld ducks, flamingoes, white nesting pelicans, and migratory ducks.

Lisar (16)

This protected zone extends over 120 sq. miles (310 sq. km) in the most western part of the Elbrus Mountains, directly above the Caspian Sea. Vegetation includes one of the last vestiges of coastal forest along the Caspian, with lime trees, oak, hornbeams, elms, maples, and ashes. Among the animals are the wolf, jackal, bear, lynx, leopard, wild boar, deer, roe buck, sheep and wild goat, and pheasant.

Central Elbrus (17)

This national park covers 784 sq. miles (2,030 sq. km) of jagged mountains, and its elevations range from sea level up to 14,355 feet (4,375 m). Forests of beechwood, hornbeam, maple, lime trees, elm, and oak grow in this park. Animal life includes wolves, bears, otters, leopards, wild cats, deer, buck, boars, wild goats and sheep, and snowcocks.

Miankaleh (18)

The peninsula of Miankaleh together with the Gorgan Bay (on the southeast bank of the Caspian) constitutes a wildlife refuge that is especially important because it serves as a winter zone for more than 250,000 aquatic birds. Among the birds that visit this peninsula are flamingoes, wild geese, the lesser white-fronted goose, small merganser, and white-headed duck. In addition, some specimens of the rare Mesopotamian doe are in specially built enclosures.

Khosh-Yeilagh (19)

Situated on the eastern Elbrus Mountains on over 580 sq. miles (1,500 sq. km) of land, this wildlife refuge includes forests of beech and oak. One can still find a small population of cheetahs and leopards, plus various species of wild cats, caracul, deer, wild boar, gazelles, Indian partridges, and snowcocks.

Eastern Elbrus (20)

This national park was founded on August 10, 1957, on nearly 355 sq. miles (920 sq. km) at the eastern edge of the Elbrus Mountains. Growing there are broad-leaved forests and steppes that are home to deer, roe buck, bears, boars, wolves, jackals, cheetahs, and leopards. In addition, there are wild sheep and many species of birds.

A caravan of nomadic shepherds crosses the eastern Iranian steppes. Even in this seemingly desolate region, typical tropical Asian wildlife reveals itself. In addition to the usual Iranian animals, species characteristic of east Indian regions are found. Because the existence of these animals depends on the few wooded areas that remain, the trees hold a position of special importance in the environment.

Miandasht (21)

The wildlife refuge of Miandasht covers 200 sq. miles (520 sq. km) between the Jajarm and Javin rivers, on the eastern borders of the Elbrus Mountains. For the most part, it contains plants that grow in salty soil, along with steppe vegetation. Cheetahs, wild jackasses, gazelles, wild sheep, cranes, bustards, and large doves are just some of the animals in this refuge.

Tandoureh (22)

Located near the border of the Soviet Union, this national park is almost 208 sq. miles (540 sq. km) in size. The park includes a mountain steppe area. The fauna includes wolves, bears, leopards, sheep, wild goats and many birds.

Touran (23)

The Touran wildlife refuge extends over 1,675 sq. miles (4,340 sq. km) at the western edge of Dasht-i-Kavir (a great salt desert), about 300 miles (500 km) east of Tehran. It covers a vast area of steppe and desert hills. The animal life includes hyenas, caracal, leopards, cheetahs, two species of gazelles (the dorcas and the goitered gazelle), and wild sheep. Of particular importance are the wild asses, which exist in great numbers in this refuge.

Kavir (24)

This national park extends over more than 2,350 sq. miles (6,090 sq. km) on the eastern margins of the Dasht-i-Kavir Desert, 105 miles (170 km), southwest of Tehran. It is comprised of sand dunes, salt flats, pebbled stretches, and rocky mountain peaks.

The vegetation includes various salty plants and arid steppe plants, such as *Aristida, Suaeda, Artemisia, Astragalus,* and tamarisk. Among the most notable animals are two species of gazelles (the gazella *edmi* and goitered gazelle), the wild ass, the cheetah, the caracal, the sheep and wild goat, and the bustard.

Oshtrankooh (25)

Situated southwest of Darud, between Qom and Ahvaz in the Zagros Mountains at an elevation of 7,000 to 13,354 feet (2,130 to 4,070 meters), this sheltered zone spreads across approximately 363 square miles (940 sq. km). It is covered by a unique kind of vegetation, which includes lentisk, almond, and juniper. Willows, cane, *Potamogeton,* algae, and mosses grow around its many small lakes.

One can observe brown bears, goats and wild sheep, bearded vultures vultures, the Caspian snowcock, sparrows, blackbirds, and Iranian and Alpine finches. Trout have been introduced in the larger lakes.

Dez and Karkheh (26)

Covering little more than 20 sq. miles (50 sq. km) in southeast Iran, these two wildlife refuges extend along the two rivers bearing the same names. The environment is dominated by the tamarisks and Euphrates poplars.

The refuge shelters the last remaining native population of Mesopotamian deer. Indian porcupines, wolves, jackels, honey badgers, wild boars, alpine grouse, and marbled ducks are found as well.

Shadegan (27)

This wildlife refuge was established on over 1,142 sq. miles (2,960 sq. km) on a vast flood plain where the Karun and five other rivers flow into the Persian Gulf. The vast marshes and mudflats become an important winter migration zone for the area's aquatic birds and animals. Among them are pelicans, white ibises, herons, little egrets, sea gulls, sea swallows, marine crustaceans, protozoa, and many ducks. Nearly half the world's population of marbled ducks dwell here.

Bakhtegan (28)

A lake with marshes and islets makes up this refuge of 1,274 sq. miles (3,300 sq. km) located to the southeast of Shiraz, 75 miles (125 km) away. Bears, hyenas, leopards, goats and wild sheep, flamingoes, and a bird known as the Italian horseman are part of the local fauna.

Khabr-va-Rouchoon (29)

Situated southeast of the Zagros Mountains, this wildlife refuge extends over about 668 sq. miles (1,730 sq. km) in a transition area between the arid steppes of the central highland and the alpine reaches 3,875 to 12,670 feet (1,181 to 3,862 m high). The fauna includes the Tibetan bear, the striped hyena, the caracal, the leopard, the sheep and wild goat, the bearded vulture, the Alpine chough, the Indian peacock, the Syrian woodpecker, and the white-cheeked bulbul.

Bazman (30)

This protected zone stretches over a little less than 1,255 sq. miles (3,250 sq. km) around Mount Zideh in southeast Iran. The vegetation, which ranges from that of the Iranian steppes to that of Sudanese steppes, comprises isolated thickets of tamarisk and groups of date palms along small streams. Groves of cane and clumps of acacia also grow. The area is situated on the border between the arctic and eastern animal regions, and beside the usual mammals found in Iran (gazelles, goats, and wild sheep), a large number of bird species thrive there.

Bahukalat (31)

Preceding page: A camel and its riders skirt the Red Sea near Elat, Israel. Aside from its famous aquarium in which Red Sea fauna live, this area is also famous as a spectacular observation point for the migratory birds that pass overhead. The predatory birds that pass over this area are of particular interest. Special camps are organized every spring to observe and track these birds.

This protected zone was established in the Sarbaz River Valley, between Firourabad and the Oman Sea, near the Pakistan border. It has characteristics of the neighboring east Indian region. Vegetation includes date palms, fan palms, tamarisks, acacias, cane, and mangroves.

Some of the animals are typically Indian, such as the palm tree squirrel, the gray mongoose, certain types of mollusks, the common maina, the sparrow hawk, and the Bengal griffin. There are also cormorants, pelicans, black storks, and a few marsh crocodiles.

Sheedvar (32)

This animal refuge was built on a small coral island 0.70 sq. miles (1.6 sq. km) in size, and is situated in the Persian Gulf. It is almost completely covered over with sand and an impenetrable shrub vegetation that grows just under 3 feet (1 m) tall. Many interesting birds make their home here, such as the little green heron, the black-throated cormorant, and the white-cheeked sea swallow. The islet is also an important nesting ground for the green turtle, one of several sea turtles threatened with extinction.

SAUDI ARABIA

Al Hassa (33)

This oasis is rich in vegetation, and spreads over 70 sq. miles (180 sq. km) in the eastern province, including the villages of Al Hufuf, Al Mubarraz, and Al Uyun. It is the dwelling place for nearly fifty mammal species, including camels, antelope, desert wolves, bats, etc. There are also eighty species of birds, such as bitterns, herons, turtledoves, bulbul, and nocturnal predatory birds.

ISRAEL

Far'un (34)

This preserve is located on a coral island in the Gulf of Elat. The rich animal life native here on its coral reef can be observed by way of an underwater viewing window. Other interesting sights along the coral reef are accessible from the street that links Elat with Sharen and Sheik. In Elat, there is a famous aquarium featuring fauna from the Red Sea.

Hai Bar (35)

This preserve of 3 sq. miles (7.2 sq. km) is nestled in the Arava Valley in the Negev Desert, and is used as a center for animal reproduction. Middle East animal species that are threatened with extinction, such as Dorcas gazelles, wild asses, ostriches, camels, wild goats, Mesopotamian deer, bezoar goats, and Arabian antelope are bred in special enclosures.

GLOSSARY

algae primitive organisms which resemble plants but do not have true roots, stems, or leaves.

amphibian any of a class of vertebrates that usually begin life in the water as tadpoles with gills and later develop lungs.

arid lacking enough water for things to grow; dry and barren.

arthropod any member of a large family of invertebrate animals with jointed legs and a segmented body.

atmosphere the gaseous mass surrounding the earth. The atmosphere consists of oxygen, nitrogen, and other gases, and extends to a height of about 22,000 miles (35,000 km).

burrow a hole or tunnel dug in the ground by an animal.

camouflage a disguise or concealment of any kind. Light-colored baby wolves of the desert camouflage themselves in the sand.

carnivore a meat-eating organism such as a predatory mammal, a bird of prey, or an insectivorous plant.

continent one of the principal land masses of the earth. Africa, Antarctica, Asia, Europe, North America, South America, and Australia are regarded as continents.

conservation the controlled use and systematic protection of natural resources, such as forests and waterways.

dormant alive, but not actually growing; in a state of suspended animation.

dromedary the one-humped or Arabian camel, that occupies the area from North Africa to India and is trained especially for fast riding.

ecology the relationship between organisms and their environment.

environment the circumstances or conditions of a plant or animal's surroundings.

ephemeral having a short life. Ephemeral plants of Western Asia adapt to the desert by having short lives.

erosion natural processes such as weathering, abrasion, and corrosion, by which material is removed from the earth's surface.

estivate to pass the summer in a dormant state.

extinction the process of destroying or extinguishing. Many species of plant and animal life face extinction either because of natural changes in the environment or those caused by carelessness.

fauna the animals of a particular region or period.

flora the plants of a specific region or time.

fossil a remnant or trace of an organism of a past geologic age, such as a skeleton or leaf imprint, embedded in some part of the earth's crust.

geology the science dealing with the physical nature and history of the earth. Geology includes a study of the structure and development of the earth's crust, the composition of its interior, individual types of rock, and the forms of life which can be found.

glaciers gigantic moving sheets of ice that covered great areas of the earth in an earlier time.

gorge a deep, narrow pass between steep heights.

habitat the area or type of environment in which a person or other organism normally exists.

herbivore an animal that eats plants.

hibernate to spend the winter in a dormant state.

invertebrate lacking a backbone or spinal column.

larva the early, immature form of any animal that changes structurally when it becomes an adult.

lichen a primitive plant formed by the association of blue-green algae with fungi.

marsh an area of low-lying flatland, such as a swamp or bog.

metamorphosis a change in form, shape, structure, or substance as a result of development.

migrate to move from one region to another with the change in seasons.

mollusk an invertebrate animal characterized by a soft, usually unsegmented body often enclosed in a shell, and having gills and a foot. Oysters, clams, and snails are mollusks.

naturalist a person who studies nature, especially by direct observation of animals and plants.

nocturnal referring to animals that are active at night.

nomads people without a permanent home, who move around constantly in search of food and pasture.

organism any individual animal or plant having diverse organs and parts that function as a whole to maintain life and its activities.

parasite an organism that grows, feeds, and is sheltered on or in a different organism while contributing nothing to the survival of its host.

physiology the branch of biology dealing with the function and processes of living organisms or their parts and organs.

raptorial predatory; of or belonging to a group of birds of prey with a strong notched beak and sharp talons, such as the eagle, hawk, or owl.

refuge shelter or protection from danger or difficulty; a place of safety.

reptile a cold-blooded vertebrate having lungs, a bony skeleton, and a body covered with scales or horny plates.

rhizome a creeping stem lying at or under the surface of the soil.

salinity of or relating to the saltiness of something.

sedimentary rocks rocks formed from sediment or from transported fragments deposited in water.

species a distinct kind, sort, variety, or class.

steppe a large plain having few trees.

symbiosis the living together of two kinds of organisms, especially where such an association provides benefits or advantages for both.

tectonic plate one of several portions of the earth's crust which has resulted from geological shifting.

terrace a raised, flat mound of earth with sloping sides.

topography the accurate and detailed description of a place.

transpiration the giving off of moisture through the surface of leaves and other parts of the plant.

ungulate of or belonging to a group of animals which have hooves.

xerophyte a plant structurally adapted to growing under very dry or desert conditions.

INDEX

CREDITS

MAPS AND DRAWINGS. G. Vaccaro, Cologna Veneta (VR). **PHOTOGRAPHY. E. Biasin—M. Marchesani,** Verona: overlap, 24. **A. Casdia—R. Massa,** Brugherio (MI): 50. **G. Corbellini,** Milan: 84. **Marka Graphic,** Milan: 72-73, 102-103; Globe Photos/J.R. Hamilton 120-121; C. Mauri 100-101, 116-117. **Novosti Press,** Rome: 86-87 **Overseas,** Milan: 89; Jacana 48; Jacana/H. Chaumeton 106; Jacana/F. Gohier 95; Jacana/J.P. Varin A. Visage 36, 38-39; Jacana/A. Visage 32; Jacana/R. Volot 55; Oxford Scientific Films/G.I. Bernard 27; Oxford Scientific Films/L. Gould 64. **Panda Photo,** Rome: Ausloos 44-45; A. Bardi 108; C. Marinucci 8, 20-21, 23; F. Petretti 47; L. Sonnino 65, 66-67, 68-69. **D. Pellegrini,** Milan: 14-15, 18-19, 29, 31, 34, 79, 80-81, 92-93. **L. Pellegrini,** Milan: 6-7, 12, 40, 60, 63, 76, 98. **F. Speranza,** Milan: A. Calegari 74-75, 77; C. Galasso 54, 57; L. Lemoine 90-91.